# Discovering
# Geometry
## An Investigative Approach

## Condensed Lessons:
## A Tool for Parents and Tutors

DISCOVERING

MATHEMATICS™

**Key Curriculum Press**
Innovators in Mathematics Education

**Teacher's Materials Project Editor:** Elizabeth DeCarli

**Project Administrator:** Brady Golden

**Writers:** David Rasmussen, Stacey Miceli

**Accuracy Checker:** Dudley Brooks

**Production Editor:** Holly Rudelitsch

**Copyeditor:** Jill Pellarin

**Editorial Production Manager:** Christine Osborne

**Production Supervisor:** Ann Rothenbuhler

**Production Coordinator:** Jennifer Young

**Text Designers:** Jenny Somerville, Garry Harman

**Composition, Technical Art, Prepress:** ICC Macmillan Inc.

**Cover Designers:** Jill Kongabel, Marilyn Perry, Jensen Barnes

**Printer:** Data Reproductions

**Textbook Product Manager:** James Ryan

**Executive Editor:** Casey FitzSimons

**Publisher:** Steven Rasmussen

Cover Photo Credits: Background image: Doug Wilson/Westlight/Corbis.
Construction site image: Sonda Dawes/The Image Works. All other images:
Ken Karp Photography.

Key Curriculum Press
1150 65th Street
Emeryville, CA 94608
510-595-7000
editorial@keypress.com
www.keypress.com

Printed in the United States of America
10 9 8 7 6 5 4 3 2      13 12 11 10 09 08      ISBN 978-1-55953-895-4

# Contents

## Chapter 5

## Chapter 6

## Chapter 7

## Chapter 8

## Chapter 9

## Chapter 10

## Chapter 11

## Chapter 12

## Chapter 13

# Introduction

Many of the key ideas in *Discovering Geometry: An Investigative Approach* are revealed through group investigations done in class. For this reason, it can be difficult for a student who has fallen behind to catch up simply by reading the student book. To provide additional support for students who have been absent or who need more time to understand new geometry concepts, two- or three-page condensed lessons have been written for most of the student lessons. These condensed lessons can also be useful as a study guide for students to use as they review, and as a resource for parents, tutors, or mentors as they work with students. Condensed lessons are not included for the optional lessons on geometric art in Chapter 0 or on tessellations in Lessons 7.6–7.8.

Each condensed lesson contains summaries of the investigations, with all the important results and their implications. In addition, most condensed lessons include worked-out examples similar to the examples in the student lesson or to an exercise in the lesson if there is no example. While there is no replacement for peer interaction or teacher guidance, reading a condensed lesson along with the lesson in the student book helps a student understand the activities and important concepts of the lesson. Students will benefit more from the condensed lessons if they work through each step of the investigations and try to solve each example before reading the solution. You might encourage students to work through the condensed lesson with a parent or friend to get the benefit of communicating ideas that they may have missed in class.

These condensed lessons can be copied two-sided to save paper. You may want to keep a file of copies handy so that they are available when you need them. Students could borrow the pages and return them to you when they complete their assignment for that lesson. Condensed lessons are also available in Spanish. Both the English and Spanish versions are available for download at www.keymath.com.

# Building Blocks of Geometry

In this lesson you will

- Learn about **points, lines,** and **planes** and how to represent them
- Learn definitions of **collinear, coplanar, line segment, congruent segments, midpoint,** and **ray**
- Learn **geometric notation** for lines, line segments, rays, and congruence

**Points, lines,** and **planes** are the building blocks of geometry. Read about these three concepts on page 28 of your book.

A **definition** is a statement that explains the meaning of a word or phrase. It is impossible to define *point, line,* and *plane* without using other words that need to be defined. For this reason, these terms remain undefined. Using these three undefined terms, you can define all other geometric figures and terms.

Keep a list of definitions in your notebook. Each time you encounter a new geometric definition, add it to your list. Illustrate each definition with a sketch. Begin your list with the definitions of **collinear, coplanar,** and **line segment** given on pages 29–30 of your book.

Make sure you understand the two ways to express the length of a segment. For example, to express the fact that the length of segment *FG* is 12 units, you can write either $FG = 12$ or $m\overline{FG} = 12$.

Two segments with equal measures, or lengths, are said to be **congruent.** The symbol for congruence is $\cong$. It is important to remember that the equals symbol, $=$, is used between equal numbers or measures, while the congruence symbol, $\cong$, is used between congruent figures.

In geometric drawings, congruent segments are marked with identical symbols. In the figure at right, $\overline{AB}$ is congruent to $\overline{DC}$. You can indicate that these segments have the same length in any of the following ways: $\overline{AB} \cong \overline{DC}$, $AB = DC$, $m\overline{AB} = m\overline{DC}$.

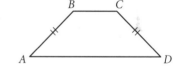

The **midpoint** of a segment is a point that divides the segment into two congruent segments. Work through the example in your book, which gives you practice identifying midpoints and congruent segments and using geometric notation. Below is another example.

**EXAMPLE** | Study the diagrams at right.

  **a.** Name each midpoint and the segment it bisects.

  **b.** Name all the congruent segments. Use the congruence symbol to write your answer.

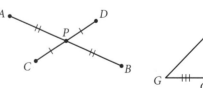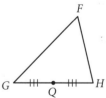

▶ **Solution** | **a.** *P* is the midpoint of both $\overline{AB}$ and $\overline{CD}$. *Q* is the midpoint of $\overline{GH}$.

   **b.** $\overline{AP} \cong \overline{PB}$, $\overline{CP} \cong \overline{PD}$, $\overline{GQ} \cong \overline{QH}$

(continued)

A **ray** is a part of a line that begins at a point and extends infinitely in one direction. A ray is named with two letters. The first letter is the endpoint, and the second letter is any other point on the ray. So ray *AB*, abbreviated $\overrightarrow{AB}$, is the part of line *AB* that contains point *A* and all the points on $\overleftrightarrow{AB}$ that are on the same side of point *A* as point *B*.

Now look back through Lesson 1.1 in your book and make sure you have recorded all the new definitions in your notebook.

## Investigation: Mathematical Models

In your book, use the photograph and the figure at the beginning of the investigation to identify examples of real-world and mathematical models for each of the following terms: point, line, plane, line segment, congruent segments, midpoint of a segment, and ray. For example, a line segment can be modeled by the top edge of a window in the photograph, and a point is modeled by the dot labeled *A* in the figure.

Now explain in your own words what each of these terms means.

# 1.2 Poolroom Math

In this lesson you will

- Learn about **angles** and how to measure them
- Identify **congruent angles** and **angle bisectors**
- Use your knowledge of angles to solve problems involving pool

An **angle** is two rays with a common endpoint, provided the two rays do not lie on the same line. The two rays are the **sides** of the angle, and the common endpoint is the **vertex.** In your book, read the text before Example A, which explains how to name angles. Then work through Example A.

The **measure of an angle** is the smallest amount of rotation about the vertex from one ray to the other. The **reflex measure of an angle** is the largest amount of rotation less than 360° between the two rays. In this course, angles are measured in **degrees.** Read the text about angle measures in your book, paying close attention to the instructions for using a **protractor.** Then use your protractor to measure the angles in Example B.

Two angles are **congruent** if and only if they have equal measures. A ray is the **angle bisector** if it contains the vertex and divides the angle into two congruent angles. In the diagram at right, $\overrightarrow{FH}$ bisects $\angle EFG$, so $\angle EFH \cong \angle GFH$. Identical markings are used to show that two angles are congruent.

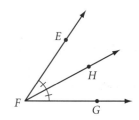

Work through Example C in your book. Here is another example.

**EXAMPLE**  |  Look for angle bisectors and congruent angles in the diagrams below.

**a.** Name each angle bisector and the angle it bisects.

**b.** Name all the congruent angles.

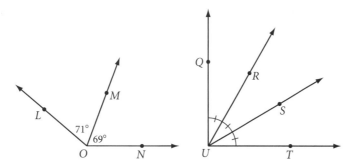

▶ **Solution**  |  **a.** $\overrightarrow{US}$ bisects $\angle RUT$. $\overrightarrow{UR}$ bisects $\angle QUS$.

**b.** $\angle SUT \cong \angle RUS \cong \angle QUR$ and $\angle QUS \cong \angle RUT$

(continued)

## Investigation: Virtual Pool

Billiards, or pool, is a game of angles. Read about **incoming angles** and **outgoing angles** in your book.

Look at the diagram of the pool table on page 42 of your book. Imagine that the ball is shot toward point $C$. The incoming angle is $\angle 1$. Use your protractor to find the measure of $\angle 1$.

The measure of the outgoing angle must equal the measure of the incoming angle. Measure $\angle BCP$ and $\angle ACP$. Which of these angles is the outgoing angle? Which point will the ball hit, point $A$ or point $B$?

Now imagine you want to hit the ball against cushion $\overleftrightarrow{WA}$ so that the ball bounces off and hits the 8-ball. Which point—$W$, $X$, or $Y$—should you hit? One way to find the answer is to measure each possible incoming angle and then check whether the ray for the congruent outgoing angle passes through the 8-ball.

Now think about how you would have to hit the ball against cushion $\overleftrightarrow{CP}$ so that it would bounce back and pass over its starting point. If you don't know, try experimenting with several different incoming angles. Each time, think about how you can adjust the angle to make the ball pass closer to its starting point.

Suppose you want to hit the ball so that it bounces off the cushions at least three times but never touches cushion $\overleftrightarrow{CP}$. Again, if you don't know, experiment. Try different incoming angles and different cushions until you start to see a pattern.

# 1.3 What's a Widget?

In this lesson you will

- Learn how to write a good definition
- Write definitions for geometric terms
- Test definitions by looking for **counterexamples**

In geometry, it is very important to be able to write clear, precise definitions.
The text on page 47 of your book discusses how to write a good definition. Read
this text carefully. Then work through Example A. Here is another example.

**EXAMPLE A** | Consider this "definition" of *rectangle:* "A rectangle is a figure with two pairs of
congruent sides."

**a.** Sketch a **counterexample.** That is, sketch a figure with two pairs of congruent
sides that is not a rectangle.

**b.** Write a better definition for *rectangle.*

▶ **Solution** | **a.** Here are two counterexamples.

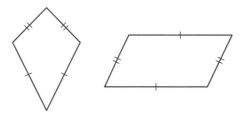

**b.** One better definition is "A rectangle is a 4-sided figure in which opposite sides
are congruent and all angles measure 90°."

Read the "Beginning Steps to Creating a Good Definition" in your book, and
make sure you understand them. Look at the symbols for parallel, perpendicular,
and 90°. Now work through Example B, which asks you to write definitions for
*parallel lines* and *perpendicular lines.*

## Investigation: Defining Angles

In this investigation you will write definitions for some important terms related
to angles.

On page 49 of your book, look at the examples of right angles and of angles
that are not right angles. What do the right angles have in common? What
characteristics do the right angles have that the other angles do not have? You
should notice that all the right angles measure 90°. The angles in the other group
have measures less than or greater than 90°. Based on this information, you could
write the following definition for *right angle.*

A **right angle** is an angle that measures 90°.

(continued)

Now look at the acute angles and the angles that are not acute. Try to use the examples to write a definition for **acute angle.** When you have written your definition, test it by trying to come up with a counterexample. When you are satisfied with your definition, look at the next set of examples, and write a definition for **obtuse angle.**

The remaining sets of examples show angle pairs. Look at the pairs of vertical angles and the pairs of angles that are not vertical angles. What do you notice? You should see that each pair of vertical angles is formed by two intersecting lines. You might start with the following definition.

Two angles are a **pair of vertical angles** if they are formed by two intersecting lines.

However, $\angle 1$ and $\angle 2$ in the "not pairs of vertical angles" group are also formed by two intersecting lines. What makes the angle pairs in the "vertical angles" group different from this pair? When you know the answer, try completing this definition.

Two angles are a **pair of vertical angles** if they are formed by two intersecting lines and _____.

Now look at the linear pairs of angles and the pairs of angles that are not linear pairs. Write a definition for **linear pair of angles.** Be sure to test your definition by looking for a counterexample. Here is one possible definition. You may have written a different definition.

Two angles are a **linear pair of angles** if they share a side and their other sides form a straight line.

Repeat this process to define **pair of complementary angles** and **pair of supplementary angles.** Think carefully about the difference between a supplementary pair and a linear pair. Make sure your definitions account for the difference.

A labeled figure can often be helpful when writing a geometric definition. Work through Example C in your book. Here is another example.

**EXAMPLE B** | Use a labeled figure to define a *vertical pair of angles.*

▶ **Solution** | $\angle AOC$ and $\angle BOD$ are a pair of vertical angles if $\overleftrightarrow{AB}$ and $\overleftrightarrow{CD}$ intersect at point $O$, and point $O$ is between points $A$ and $B$ and also between points $C$ and $D$.

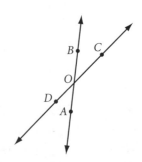

In the definition, is it necessary to state that point $O$ is between the other two points on each line? Sketch a counterexample that shows why this part of the definition is necessary.

Add definitions for all the new terms in this lesson to your definition list. Be sure to include a sketch with each definition.

## CONDENSED LESSON

# 1.4 Polygons

In this lesson you will

- Learn the definition of **polygon**
- Learn the meaning of terms associated with polygons, such as **concave, convex, equilateral, equiangular,** and **regular**
- Identify **congruent polygons**

A **polygon** is a closed figure in a plane, formed by connecting line segments endpoint to endpoint with each segment intersecting exactly two others.

Look closely at the examples of "polygons" and "not polygons" on page 54 of your book. Check that each figure in the "polygons" group fits the definition. Then try to explain why each figure in the "not polygons" group is not a polygon.

Each line segment in a polygon is a **side** of a polygon. Each endpoint where the sides meet is a **vertex** of the polygon.

Polygons are classified by the number of sides they have. The chart on page 54 of your book gives the names of polygons with different numbers of sides.

You name a polygon by listing the vertices in consecutive order. It does not matter which vertex you start with. For example, you could name this polygon quadrilateral *PQRS* or *RQPS*, but not *PRQS*. When you name a triangle, you can use the △ symbol. For example, △*XYZ* means triangle *XYZ*.

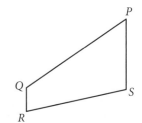

A **diagonal** of a polygon is a line segment that connects two *nonconsecutive* vertices. A polygon is **convex** if no diagonal is outside the polygon. A polygon is **concave** if at least one diagonal is outside the polygon. See page 54 of your book for more examples of convex and concave polygons.

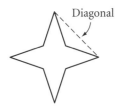

Diagonal    Diagonal

Convex polygon

Concave polygon

Two polygons are **congruent polygons** if and only if they are exactly the same size and shape. If two polygons are congruent, then their corresponding angles and sides are congruent. For example, triangle *ABC* is congruent to triangle *EFG*, so their three pairs of corresponding angles and three pairs of corresponding sides are also congruent.

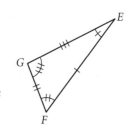

$\angle A \cong \angle E$      $\angle B \cong \angle F$      $\angle C \cong \angle G$

$\overline{AB} \cong \overline{EF}$      $\overline{BC} \cong \overline{FG}$      $\overline{CA} \cong \overline{GE}$

When you write a statement of congruence, always write the letters of the corresponding vertices in an order that shows the correspondence. For example, when referring to the triangles at right, the statements △*ABC* ≅ △*EFG* and △*CAB* ≅ △*GEF* are correct, but △*ABC* ≅ △*FEG* is incorrect.

(continued)

**EXAMPLE** | Which polygon is congruent to *TUVW*?

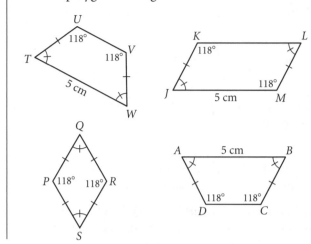

▶ **Solution** | Polygon *TUVW* ≅ polygon *BCDA*. You could also say *TUVW* ≅ *ADCB*.

The **perimeter** of a polygon is the sum of the lengths of its sides. The perimeter of the polygon at right is 28 cm.

## Investigation: Special Polygons

In this investigation you will write definitions for three special polygons.

In your book, look at the polygons that are equilateral and the polygons that are not equilateral. What characteristics do the equilateral polygons have that the other polygons don't have? You should notice that in each equilateral polygon all sides have equal length, whereas in a polygon that is not equilateral, not all sides have equal length. From this observation you could write the following definition:

An equilateral polygon is a polygon in which all sides have equal length.

Now look at the polygons that are equiangular and the polygons that are not equiangular. Use the examples to write a definition of **equiangular polygon.**

Finally, look at the polygons that are regular polygons and the ones that are not regular polygons. Decide which characteristics separate the polygons into the two groups and write a definition of **regular polygon.** Your definition might be in this form:

A regular polygon is a polygon that is both _____ and _____.

Add definitions for all the new terms in this lesson to your definition list. Be sure to include a sketch with each definition.

# CONDENSED LESSON 1.5 Triangles

In this lesson you will

- Learn how to interpret geometric diagrams
- Write definitions for types of triangles

When you look at a geometric diagram, you must be careful not to assume too much from it. For example, you should *not* assume that two segments that appear to be the same length actually are the same length, unless they are marked as congruent.

You may assume

that lines are straight and if two lines intersect they intersect at one point.

that all points on a line are collinear and all points on a diagram are coplanar unless planes are drawn to show they are noncoplanar.

You may not assume

that lines are parallel unless they are marked as parallel.

that lines are perpendicular unless they are marked as perpendicular.

that pairs of angles, segments, or polygons are congruent unless they are marked with information that tells you they are congruent.

**EXAMPLE**

In the figure below, which pairs of lines are parallel? Which pairs of lines are perpendicular? Which pairs of triangles are congruent?

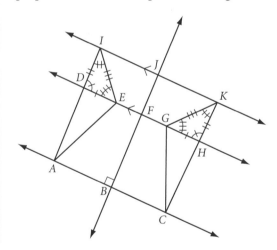

▶ **Solution**

Lines *IJ* and *EG* are parallel. Lines *BF* and *AC* are perpendicular. Triangles *IDE* and *KHG* are congruent.

(continued)

## Investigation: Triangles

In this investigation, you will write definitions for types of triangles.

In your book, look at the right triangles and the figures that are not right triangles. What do the right triangles have in common? What characteristics do the right triangles have that the other triangles do not have? You should notice that all the right triangles have a right angle (an angle that measures 90°). None of the other triangles have a right angle. Based on this information, you could write the following definition for a right triangle.

A **right triangle** is a triangle with one right angle.

Now, look at the acute triangles and the triangles that are not acute.

Use the examples to write a definition for **acute triangle.** When you have written your definition, test it by trying to come up with a counterexample. When you are satisfied with your definition, look at the next set of examples, and write a definition for **obtuse triangle.**

Look back at your definitions of *right triangle, acute triangle,* and *obtuse triangle.* If you have written correct definitions, any triangle you are given will fit *one and only one* of these definitions. Check that each triangle below fits one and only one of your definitions. If not, go back and refine your definitions.

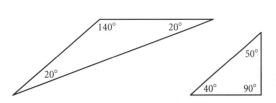 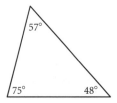

Look at the next three sets of examples, and write definitions for **scalene triangle, equilateral triangle,** and **isosceles triangle.** (Hint: Focus on the side lengths of the triangles.) If your definitions are correct, any triangle will fit one and only one of these definitions. Draw several triangles and test each one to make sure this is true. If it is not, refine your definitions.

In an isosceles triangle, the angle between the two sides of equal length is called the **vertex angle.** The side opposite the vertex angle is called the **base** of the isosceles triangle. The two angles opposite the two sides of equal length are called **base angles** of the isosceles triangle.

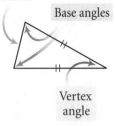

Add the definition for each type of triangle to your definition list. Be sure to include a labeled drawing with each definition.

# 1.6 Special Quadrilaterals

In this lesson you will

- Write definitions for special types of quadrilaterals

All of the quadrilaterals in this lesson can be made by attaching two congruent triangles along a corresponding side. Depending on the type of triangles you join, the quadrilaterals have different properties. In the following investigation you will define different types of special quadrilaterals based on relationships of their sides and angles.

## Investigation: Special Quadrilaterals

On page 64 of your book, look at the figures that are trapezoids and the figures that are not trapezoids. What differentiates the trapezoids from the nontrapezoids? Each trapezoid is a figure with a pair of parallel sides. So, you might start with this definition.

A **trapezoid** is a figure with a pair of parallel sides.

However, two of the figures in the "not trapezoids" group also have a pair of parallel sides. One of these figures has two pairs of parallel sides, while all the trapezoids have only one pair. So, you could refine the definition like this.

A **trapezoid** is a figure with exactly one pair of parallel sides.

This definition is better, but one of the nontrapezoids satisfies it. Notice, though, that this nontrapezoid has five sides, while each trapezoid has four sides. You can refine the definition once again.

A **trapezoid** is a quadrilateral with exactly one pair of parallel sides.

This definition fits all the trapezoids and none of the nontrapezoids.

Now write definitions for the next two terms, **kite** and **parallelogram.** Note that these figures have some things in common, but there are also important differences between them. Make sure your definitions account for these differences.

Move on to write definitions for **rhombus, rectangle,** and **square.** There are several correct definitions for each of these terms. Once you define a term, you can use it in the definition for another term. For example, a rhombus is a special type of parallelogram, so your definition might be in this form.

A **rhombus** is a parallelogram with _____.

A square is a special type of rhombus *and* a special type of rectangle, so your definition might be in one of the following forms.

A **square** is a rhombus with _____.

A **square** is a rectangle with _____.

Here is another possible definition.

A **square** is a rhombus that is also a rectangle.

(continued)

Add the definition for each type of quadrilateral to your definition list. Be sure to
include a labeled drawing with each definition.

**EXAMPLE**

Look carefully at the quadrilaterals. Classify each figure as a trapezoid, kite,
rhombus, rectangle, or square. Explain your thinking.

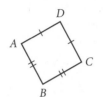

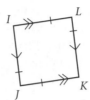
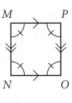

▶ **Solution**

Quadrilateral *ABCD* is a kite because two pairs of adjacent sides are congruent.
Quadrilateral *EFGH* is a trapezoid because it has only one pair of parallel sides.
Quadrilateral *IJKL* is a rhombus because it is a parallelogram and all of its sides
have equal length. Quadrilateral *MNOP* is a rectangle because it is a parallelogram
and all of its angles have equal measures.

# 1.7  Circles

In this lesson you will

- Learn the definition of **circle**
- Write definitions for **chord, diameter,** and **tangent**
- Learn about three types of **arcs** and how they are measured

A **circle** is the set of all points in a plane that are a given distance from a given point. The given distance is called the **radius** and the given point is called the **center.** The word *radius* is also used to refer to a segment from the center to a point on the circle. You name a circle by its center. The circle below is circle *P.*

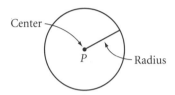

The **diameter** of a circle is a line segment containing the center, with its endpoints on the circle. The word *diameter* is also used to refer to the length of this segment.

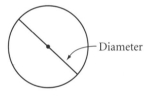

## Investigation: Defining Circle Terms

In this investigation you will write definitions for terms associated with circles.

In your book, look at the examples of chords and nonchords. What do the chords have in common? What characteristics do the chords have that the nonchords do not? For example, the chords are all segments, and each chord has two points on the circle. One of the nonchords, namely $\overline{RS}$, also has these properties. However, each chord has *both endpoints* on the circle, while $\overline{RS}$ has only one of its endpoints on the circle. Using these observations, you could write this definition.

A **chord** of a circle is a segment with both of its endpoints on the circle.

Now study the examples of diameters and nondiameters. Use your observations to write a definition for *diameter.* Because you have already defined *chord,* you can use this term in your definition. Your definition might be in one of the following forms.

A **diameter** of a circle is a segment that _____.

A **diameter** of a circle is a chord that _____.

Finally, study the examples of tangents and nontangents, and use your observations to define **tangent.** Be sure to check your definition by looking

(continued)

for a counterexample. Note that the point where the tangent touches the circle is called the **point of tangency.**

Look at the questions in Steps 2 and 3 in your book. Make sure you can answer these questions. Think about the definitions you wrote in Step 1 and how they are similar and different.

**Congruent circles** are circles with the same radius. **Concentric circles** are circles in the same plane with the same center.

Congruent circles          Concentric circles

An **arc of a circle** is two points on the circle and the continuous (unbroken) part of the circle between the two points. Arcs can be classified into three types. A **semicircle** is an arc of a circle whose endpoints are on a diameter. A **minor arc** is an arc that is smaller than a semicircle. A **major arc** is an arc that is larger than a semicircle. You name a minor arc with the letters of its endpoints. You name semicircles and major arcs with the letters of three points—the first and last letters are the endpoints, and the middle letter is any other point on the arc. See the diagram on page 71 of your book for examples of each type of arc.

Arcs are measured in degrees. A full circle has an arc measure of 360°, a semicircle has an arc measure of 180°, and so on. The measure of a minor arc is equal to the measure of the *central angle* associated with the arc. The **central angle** is the angle with its vertex at the center of the circle and its sides passing through the endpoints of the arc.

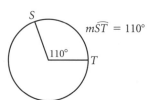

$m\widehat{ST} = 110°$

Add definitions for all the new terms in this lesson to your definition list. Be sure to include a labeled drawing with each definition.

# Space Geometry

In this lesson you will

- Learn the mathematical definition of **space**
- Learn the names of common three-dimensional objects and how to draw them
- Solve problems that require you to visualize objects in space

The work you have done so far has involved objects in a single plane. In this lesson you will need to visualize objects in three dimensions, or space. Read about space on page 75 of your book.

In geometry, it is important to be able to recognize three-dimensional objects from two-dimensional drawings, and to create drawings that represent three-dimensional objects. Pages 75–77 in your book show examples of common three-dimensional objects and give tips for drawing these objects. Read this text carefully and practice drawing the objects.

## Investigation: Space Geometry

In this investigation you need to decide whether statements about geometric objects are true or false. You can make sketches or use physical objects to help you visualize each statement. For example, you might use a sheet of paper to represent a plane and a pencil to represent a line. In each case, try to find a counterexample to the statement. If you find one, the statement must be false. If a statement is false, draw a picture and explain why it is false.

Below are some suggestions for visualizing the situations described in the statements. Try to determine whether each statement is true or false on your own before you read the suggestion.

1. For any two points, there is exactly one line that can be drawn through them.

   Draw two points on a sheet of paper and draw a line through them. Is there a way to draw another straight line through the points? Remember that you are not limited to the surface of the paper.

2. For any line and a point not on the line, there is exactly one plane that contains them.

   Draw a dot on a sheet of paper to represent the point, and use a pencil to represent the line. Hold the pencil above the paper and imagine a plane passing through both the point and the line.

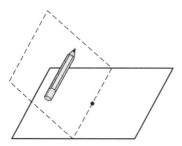

(continued)

Without moving the point or the line, try to imagine a different plane passing through them. Can you do it? Change the position of the pencil and the paper so that they represent a different point and line. Can you imagine more than one plane passing through them? Experiment until you think you know whether the statement is true or false.

**3.** For any two lines, there is exactly one plane that contains them.

There are three situations that you must consider: intersecting lines, parallel lines, and skew lines.

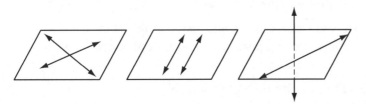

First, look at the intersecting lines. They are drawn on a sheet of paper, which can represent a plane containing the lines. Try to imagine a different plane that also contains both lines. Can you do it?

Next, study the parallel lines contained in the plane of the sheet of paper. Can a different plane contain both parallel lines? Finally, look at the third pair of lines, which are skew lines, or lines that are not parallel and do not intersect. Can you imagine a sheet of paper that will contain these lines?

**4.** If two coplanar lines are both perpendicular to a third line in the same plane, then the two lines are parallel.

Notice that all the lines mentioned in this statement are in the same plane. You can use a sheet of paper to represent the plane. On the paper, draw a line and then draw two lines that are each perpendicular to the line. Are the two lines parallel? Make more sketches if you need to.

**5.** If two planes do not intersect, then they are parallel.

Use two sheets of paper or cardboard to represent the planes. You'll need to picture the sheets extending forever. Can you arrange the planes so that they will never intersect but so they are *not* parallel?

**6.** If two lines do not intersect, then they are parallel.

You know that if lines *in the same plane* do not intersect, then they must be parallel. But what if the lines are in different planes? You can use two pencils to represent two lines. See if you can position the lines so that they will not intersect and are *not* parallel.

**7.** If a line is perpendicular to two lines in a plane, but the line is not contained in the plane, then the line is perpendicular to the plane.

You can use a sheet of paper to represent the plane. Draw two lines on the paper to represent the two lines in the plane. The third line is not contained in the plane. Represent this line with a pencil. Hold the pencil so that it is perpendicular to both of the lines in the plane. (Note: In order for you to do this, the lines in the plane must intersect.)

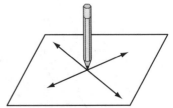

Is the pencil perpendicular to the plane? Experiment until you are convinced you know whether the statement is true or false.

# A Picture Is Worth a Thousand Words

In this lesson you will

- Solve problems that require visual thinking
- Draw diagrams to help you solve problems

When you are solving a problem that requires you to visualize something, it often helps to draw a diagram. In the examples in this lesson, you will apply your visualization skills to solve problems. Work through all the examples in your book, using diagrams to help you find the solutions. Below are some additional examples. Try to solve each problem yourself before looking at the solution.

**EXAMPLE A**  Five friends rode in a 50-mile bike race. Sue finished 25 minutes after Ana. Ana finished 40 minutes before Mel. Mel finished 25 minutes after Jing. Rosi finished 20 minutes before Jing. If Ana finished at 1:30 P.M., what time did each of the other girls finish?

▶ **Solution**  You can plot the information, one fact at a time, on a "time line."

Sue finished 25 minutes after Ana.

Ana                    Sue
●—————————————●
       25 min

Ana finished 40 minutes before Mel.

Ana                    Sue           Mel
●—————————————●—————————●
       25 min              15 min

Mel finished 25 minutes after Jing.

Ana          Jing      Sue           Mel
●——————●——————●—————————●
   15 min     10 min       15 min

Rosi finished 20 minutes before Jing.

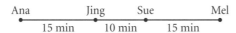

Rosi  Ana            Jing      Sue           Mel
●———●——————●——————●—————————●
 5 min   15 min     10 min       15 min

Use the fact that Ana finished at 1:30 P.M., along with the information on the time line, to figure out when each girl finished.

Rosi: 1:25 P.M.     Jing: 1:45 P.M.     Sue: 1:55 P.M.     Mel: 2:10 P.M.

In the next example, you need to identify a **locus** of points.

**EXAMPLE B**  Oak Street and Maple Street are perpendicular to one another. Maya and Chris are looking for their lost dog. Maya is on Oak Street, 50 meters north of the corner of Oak and Maple. Chris is on Maple Street, 70 meters east of the corner. The dog is 60 meters from Maya and 50 meters from Chris. Make a diagram showing the places where the dog might be located.

(continued)

▶ **Solution** | Start by drawing a diagram showing the two streets and the locations of Maya and Chris. Because the dog is 60 meters from Maya, draw a circle with radius 60 meters centered at point *M*. Because the dog is 50 meters from Chris, draw a circle with radius 50 meters centered at point *C*. The intersection of the circles marks the two places the dog might be.

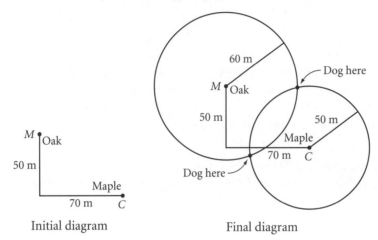

Initial diagram

Final diagram

A Venn diagram is a large circle (or oval) that contains smaller circles (or ovals). The large circle represents a whole collection of things, and the smaller circles represent special parts (or subsets) of the whole collection.

**EXAMPLE C** | Create a Venn diagram showing the relationships among polygons, equilateral polygons, equiangular polygons, and regular polygons.

▶ **Solution** | The large circle in your Venn diagram must represent what polygons, equilateral polygons, equiangular polygons, and regular polygons all have in common. All of these are polygons. So, the large outer circle represents polygons.

An equilateral polygon is a special polygon with all sides the same length. So, a small inner circle can represent equilateral polygons.

An equiangular polygon is a special polygon in which all angles have equal measures. Therefore, a second small inner circle can represent equiangular polygons.

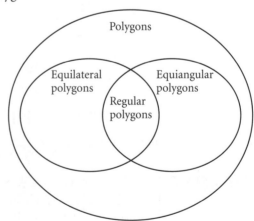

The intersection of the two inner circles represents polygons that are both equilateral and equiangular. This is the definition of a regular polygon.

The Venn diagram at right can visually represent the relationships among these figures.

*Discovering Geometry Condensed Lessons*
©2008 Key Curriculum Press

# Inductive Reasoning

In this lesson you will

- Learn how **inductive reasoning** is used in science and mathematics
- Use inductive reasoning to make **conjectures** about sequences of numbers and shapes

**Inductive reasoning** is the process of observing data, recognizing patterns, and making generalizations based on those patterns. You probably use inductive reasoning all the time without realizing it. For example, suppose your history teacher likes to give "surprise" quizzes. You notice that, for the first four chapters of the book, she gave a quiz the day after she covered the third lesson. Based on the pattern in your observations, you might generalize that you will have a quiz after the third lesson of every chapter. A generalization based on inductive reasoning is called a **conjecture.**

Example A in your book gives an example of how inductive reasoning is used in science. Here is another example.

**EXAMPLE A**
In physics class, Dante's group dropped a ball from different heights and measured the height of the first bounce. They recorded their results in this table.

| Drop height (cm) | 120 | 100 | 160 | 40 | 200 | 80 |
| --- | --- | --- | --- | --- | --- | --- |
| First-bounce height (cm) | 90 | 74 | 122 | 30 | 152 | 59 |

Make a conjecture based on their findings. Then predict the first-bounce height for a drop height of 280 cm.

▶ **Solution**
If you divide each first-bounce height by the corresponding drop height, you get the following results: 0.75, 0.74, 0.7625, 0.75, 0.76, 0.7375. Based on these results, you could make this conjecture: "For this ball, the height of the first bounce will always be about 75% of the drop height."

Based on this conjecture, the first-bounce height for a drop height of 280 cm would be about $280 \cdot 0.75$, or 210 cm.

Example B in your book illustrates how inductive reasoning can be used to make a conjecture about a number sequence. Here is another example.

**EXAMPLE B**
Consider the sequence

10, 7, 9, 6, 8, 5, 7, . . .

Make a conjecture about the rule for generating the sequence. Then find the next three terms.

(continued)

▶ **Solution** | Look at how the numbers change from term to term.

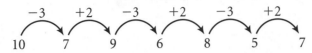

The 1st term in the sequence is 10. You subtract 3 to get the 2nd term. Then you add 2 to get the 3rd term. You continue alternating between subtracting 3 and adding 2 to generate the remaining terms. The next three terms are 4, 6, and 3.

In the investigation you look at a pattern in a sequence of shapes.

## Investigation: Shape Shifters

Look at the sequence of shapes in the investigation in your book. Complete each step of the investigation. Below are hints for each step if you need them.

**Step 1**  Are the shapes the same or different? How does the shaded portion of the shape change from one odd-numbered shape to the next?

**Step 2**  First, focus on the polygon shape. Does the polygon change from one even-numbered shape to the next? If so, how does it change? Second, focus on the small circles inside the shape. How do these circles change from one even-numbered shape to the next?

**Step 3**  The next shape is the 7th shape. Because it is an odd-numbered shape, use the patterns you described in Step 1 to figure out what it will look like. The 8th shape is an even-numbered shape, so it should follow the patterns you described in Step 2.

**Step 4**  Notice that the odd-numbered shapes go through a cycle that repeats every eight terms. So, for example, the 1st, 9th, and 17th shapes look the same; the 3rd, 11th, and 19th shapes look the same; and so on. Use this idea to figure out what the 25th shape looks like.

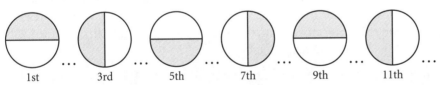

1st      3rd      5th      7th      9th      11th

**Step 5**  How many sides does the 2nd shape have? The 4th shape? The 6th shape? The $n$th shape? How many sides will the 30th shape have? How will the dots be arranged on the 30th shape?

Read the text following the investigation in your book.

*Discovering Geometry Condensed Lessons*
©2008 Key Curriculum Press

# Finding the *n*th Term

In this lesson you will

- Learn how to write **function rules** for number sequences with a constant difference
- Write a rule to describe a geometric pattern
- Learn why a rule for a sequence with a constant difference is called a **linear function**

Consider the sequence 20, 27, 34, 41, 48, 55, 62, . . . . Notice that the difference between any two consecutive terms is 7. We say that this sequence has a *constant difference* of 7. To find the next two terms in the sequence, you could add 7 to the last term to get 69, and then add 7 to 69 to get 76. But what if you wanted to find the 200th term? It would take a long time to list all the terms. If you could find a rule for calculating the *n*th term of the sequence for any number *n*, you could find the 200th term without having to list all the terms before it. This rule is called the **function rule.** In the investigation you will learn a method for writing a rule for any sequence that has a constant difference.

## Investigation: Finding the Rule

Copy and complete each table in Step 1 of the investigation. Then find the difference between consecutive values. If the difference is constant, look for a connection between the difference and the rule.

Here is the completed table for part c. Notice that the values have a constant difference of $-2$, which is equal to the coefficient of $n$ in the rule $-2n + 5$.

| $n$ | 1 | 2 | 3 | 4 | 5 | 6 | 7 | 8 |
|---|---|---|---|---|---|---|---|---|
| $-2n + 5$ | 3 | 1 | $-1$ | $-3$ | $-5$ | $-7$ | $-9$ | $-11$ |

$$-2 \quad -2 \quad -2 \quad -2 \quad -2 \quad -2 \quad -2$$

For each table, you should have found a constant difference and observed that the constant difference is equal to the coefficient of $n$ in the rule. If you didn't, go back and check your work. In general, if the difference between consecutive terms in a sequence is a constant value $a$, then the coefficient of $n$ in the rule is $a$.

Now return to the sequence 20, 27, 34, 41, 48, 55, 62, . . . from the beginning of the lesson. You can organize the terms in a table.

| Term $n$ | 1 | 2 | 3 | 4 | 5 | 6 | 7 | . . . | 200 |
|---|---|---|---|---|---|---|---|---|---|
| Value $f(n)$ | 20 | 27 | 34 | 41 | 48 | 55 | 62 | . . . | |

The constant difference for this sequence is 7, so you know that part of the rule is $7n$. The value of the first term ($n = 1$) of the sequence is 20. Substituting 1 for $n$ in $7n$ gives $7(1) = 7$. To get 20, you need to add 13. So, the rule is $7n + 13$.

(continued)

Check this rule by trying it for other terms of the sequence. For example, when $n = 4$, $7n + 13 = 28 + 13 = 41$, which is the 4th term in the sequence.

You can use the rule to find the 200th term in the sequence. The 200th term is $7(200) + 13$, or 1413.

To get more practice writing rules for patterns, work through Examples A and B in your book. Below is another example.

**EXAMPLE** | If the pattern of T-shapes continues, how many squares will be in the 100th T-shape?

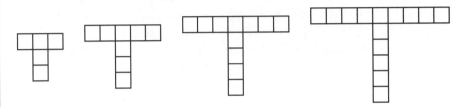

▶ **Solution** | Make a table showing the number of squares in each of the T-shapes shown.

| T-shape | 1 | 2 | 3 | 4 | . . . | *n* | . . . | 100 |
|---|---|---|---|---|---|---|---|---|
| Number of squares | 5 | 8 | 11 | 14 | . . . | | . . . | |

Now try to find a rule for the number of squares in the *n*th T-shape. Because the constant difference is 3, the rule is of the form $3n + c$. Because the number of squares in the first shape ($n = 1$) is 5, $c = 2$. The rule is $3n + 2$. Therefore, there are $3(100) + 2$, or 302, squares in the 100th T-shape.

In the T-shape example, the process of looking at patterns and generalizing a rule for the *n*th shape is inductive reasoning. The rule found in this example is called a **linear function.** A linear function is a rule that generates a sequence with a constant difference.

To see why the rule in the T-shape example is a linear function, you can graph the value for the sequence as ordered pairs of the form (*term number, value*) on the coordinate plane. The points on your graph will be collinear, because each time the term number increases by 1, the value goes up by the constant difference 3. The line $y = 3x + 2$ passes through the points.

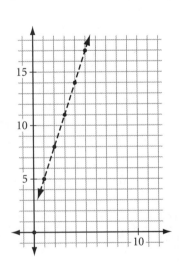

# 2.3 Mathematical Modeling

**CONDENSED LESSON**

In this lesson you will

- Attempt to solve a problem by **acting it out**
- Create a **mathematical model** for a problem
- Learn about **triangular numbers** and the formula for generating them

When you represent a situation with a graph, diagram, or equation, you are creating a **mathematical model.** Suppose you throw a ball straight up into the air with an initial velocity of 60 ft/s. You may recall from algebra that if you release the ball from a height of 5 ft, then the height $h$ of the ball after $t$ seconds can be modeled with the equation and graph shown at right. Once you have created a model, you can use it to make predictions. For example, you could use the equation or graph to predict the height of the ball after 2 seconds or to predict when the ball will hit the ground.

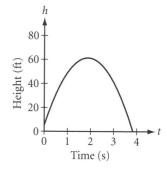

$$h = -16t^2 + 60t + 5$$

In the investigation you will solve a problem by creating mathematical models.

## Investigation: Party Handshakes

If each of the 30 people at a party shook hands with everyone else, how many handshakes were there altogether?

If you can gather a group of four people, act out the problem for "parties" of one, two, three, and four people and record your results in a table. Your table should look like this.

| People | 1 | 2 | 3 | 4 | . . . | 30 |
|---|---|---|---|---|---|---|
| Handshakes | 0 | 1 | 3 | 6 | . . . | |

Can you generalize from your table to find the number of handshakes for 30 people? It would certainly help if you had more data. However, gathering many people to act out the problem is not very practical. You could instead try using a mathematical model.

Model the problem by using points to represent people and line segments connecting the points to represent handshakes.

1 person        2 people        3 people        4 people
0 handshakes    1 handshake     3 handshakes    6 handshakes

Record your results in a table. This table gives the results for up to six people, but you may want to find results for larger groups of people to help you find a pattern.

| Number of points (people) | 1 | 2 | 3 | 4 | 5 | 6 | . . . | $n$ | . . . | 30 |
|---|---|---|---|---|---|---|---|---|---|---|
| Number of segments (handshakes) | 0 | 1 | 3 | 6 | 10 | 15 | . . . | | . . . | |

                                    1   2   3   4   5

Notice that the pattern does not have a constant difference, so the rule is not a linear function.

(continued)

Read the dialogue between Erin and Stephanie in your book. According to Erin and Stephanie's line of reasoning, the diagram with 5 points should have 4 segments per point, so the total number of segments should be $\frac{5 \cdot 4}{2}$, or 10. This matches the data in the table.

Copy and complete the table given in Step 6 in your book. Make sure you can answer these questions about the expressions for the number of handshakes.

- What does the larger of the two factors in each numerator represent?
- What does the smaller factor represent?
- Why is the product of the factors divided by 2?

You should find that the rule $\frac{n(n-1)}{2}$ models the number of handshakes for a group of $n$ people. So, for 30 people, there would be $\frac{30 \cdot 29}{2}$, or 435, handshakes.

The numbers in the pattern in the investigation are called **triangular numbers** because you can represent them with a triangular pattern of points.

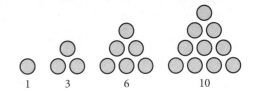

1     3     6     10

Read the text after the investigation in your book, which shows how you can derive a formula for the triangular numbers using **rectangular numbers**. As expected, the formula is the same one you found in the investigation. Here is another example of a handshake problem.

**EXAMPLE** | Before a soccer game, each of the 11 players on one team shook hands with each player on the other team. How many handshakes were there?

▶ **Solution** | Draw diagrams to represent this situation for teams of one, two, three, and four players, and record the results in a table. (Keep in mind that the players do *not* shake hands with members of their own team.)

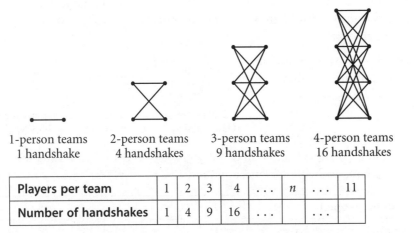

1-person teams     2-person teams     3-person teams     4-person teams
1 handshake        4 handshakes       9 handshakes       16 handshakes

| Players per team | 1 | 2 | 3 | 4 | ... | $n$ | ... | 11 |
|---|---|---|---|---|---|---|---|---|
| Number of handshakes | 1 | 4 | 9 | 16 | ... | | | ... |

Do you see a pattern? In each case, the number of handshakes is the square of the number of people on each team. The rule for the number of handshakes between two $n$-player teams is $n^2$. So, for the 11-player soccer teams, there were $11^2$, or 121, handshakes.

# Deductive Reasoning

In this lesson you will

- Learn about **deductive reasoning**
- Use deductive reasoning to justify the steps in the solution of an equation
- Use a deductive argument to explain why a geometric conjecture is true

In Lessons 2.1–2.3, you used inductive reasoning to make conjectures based on observed patterns. To explain *why* a conjecture is true, you need to use *deductive* reasoning. **Deductive reasoning** is the process of showing that certain statements follow logically from accepted facts. Read about deductive reasoning on page 114 of your book.

When you give a reason for each step in the process of solving an equation, you are using deductive reasoning. Example A in your book shows the steps involved in solving a particular algebraic equation. Here is another example.

**EXAMPLE**  Solve the equation for $x$. Give a reason for each step in the solution process.

$$5x^2 + 19x - 45 = 5x(x + 2)$$

▶ **Solution**  

| | |
|---|---|
| $5x^2 + 19x - 45 = 5x(x + 2)$ | The original equation. |
| $5x^2 + 19x - 45 = 5x^2 + 10x$ | Distribute. |
| $19x - 45 = 10x$ | Subtract $5x^2$ from both sides. |
| $-45 = -9x$ | Subtract $19x$ from both sides. |
| $5 = x$ | Divide both sides by $-9$. |

Read Example B in your book carefully. It shows three examples of a ray bisecting an obtuse angle. In each case, the two newly formed congruent angles are acute. From these examples, *inductive reasoning* is used to form the following conjecture.

If an obtuse angle is bisected, then the two newly formed congruent angles are acute.

Once the conjecture is stated, a *deductive argument* is used to show it is true. Notice that, by using a variable, $m$, to represent the measure of an obtuse angle, the argument shows that the conjecture is true for *any* obtuse angle. As another example of using a deductive argument to explain why a conjecture is true, consider the three obtuse angles in Example B of your book with their bisector, $\overrightarrow{AC}$. This time make a conjecture which states the minimum angle measure for each of the newly formed congruent angles. Looking again at the measures of the new angles—60°, 79°, and 46°—you notice that each is larger than 45°. So, one possible conjecture is stated here.

**Conjecture:** If an obtuse angle is bisected, then the two newly formed congruent angles have measures greater than 45°.

(continued)

Complete the following deductive argument to show that this conjecture is true.

**Deductive Argument:** Let $a$ be the measure of an obtuse angle.

$$a > \underline{\hspace{2cm}}$$

When an angle is bisected, the newly formed angles each measure half the original angle.

$$\frac{1}{2}a > \underline{\hspace{2cm}}$$

Therefore, the newly formed congruent angles have measures greater than 45°.

In the investigation you will use inductive reasoning to form a conjecture and deductive reasoning to explain why it is true.

## Investigation: Overlapping Segments

Look at the two diagrams at the beginning of the investigation. In each diagram, $\overline{AB} \cong \overline{CD}$.

For each diagram, find the lengths of $\overline{AC}$ and $\overline{BD}$. What do you notice? You should find that in each case $\overline{AC} \cong \overline{BD}$.

Now draw your own segment $AD$. Place points $B$ and $C$ on the segment so that $\overline{AB} \cong \overline{CD}$ and $B$ is closer to point $A$ than to point $D$. Measure $\overline{AC}$ and $\overline{BD}$. You should find that, as in the diagrams in the investigation, $\overline{AC} \cong \overline{BD}$.

Use your findings to complete the conjecture that is started in the book in Step 4. Your completed conjecture should be similar to this one:

If $\overline{AD}$ has points $A$, $B$, $C$, and $D$ in that order with $\overline{AB} \cong \overline{CD}$, then the overlapping segments $AC$ and $BD$ are congruent (that is, $\overline{AC} \cong \overline{BD}$).

This conjecture is known as the overlapping segments property. Now write a deductive argument to explain why the conjecture is true. (Hint: Use the facts that $\overline{BC}$ is a part of both $\overline{AC}$ and $\overline{BD}$ and that the other parts of $\overline{AC}$ and $\overline{BD}$—namely, $\overline{AB}$ and $\overline{CD}$—are congruent.) After you have written your own deductive argument, compare it to the one below.

**Deductive Argument:** Because $\overline{AB} \cong \overline{CD}$, you know that

$$AB = CD$$

You can add the same thing to both sides of an equation and the equation remains true.

$$AB + BC = BC + CD$$

Using segment addition, $AB + BC = AC$ and $BC + CD = BD$. By substituting $AC$ for $AB + BC$ and $BD$ for $BC + CD$ in the equation above, you get the following:

$$AC = BD$$

By the definition of congruent segments, $\overline{AC} \cong \overline{BD}$.

Read the text following the investigation in your book.

# Angle Relationships

In this lesson you will

- Make a conjecture about angles that form a **linear pair**
- Make and prove a conjecture about pairs of **vertical angles**
- Write the **converse** of an "if-then" statement and determine whether it is true

In this lesson you will use inductive reasoning to discover some geometric relationships involving angles.

## Investigation 1: The Linear Pair Conjecture

Repeat Step 1 of Investigation 1 three times, creating three different pairs of linear angles.

You should find that, for each pair of linear angles, the sum of the angle measures is 180°. This discovery leads to the following conjecture.

> **Linear Pair Conjecture** If two angles form a linear pair, then the measures    **C-1**
> of the angles add up to 180°.

Keep a list of important conjectures in your notebook. Make a sketch for each conjecture. The Linear Pair Conjecture (C-1) should be the first entry in your list.

## Investigation 2: Vertical Angles Conjecture

Follow Steps 1–3 in your book. You should find that the vertical angles are congruent. That is, $\angle 1 \cong \angle 3$ and $\angle 2 \cong \angle 4$.

Now draw a different pair of intersecting lines on patty paper and repeat Steps 2 and 3. Are the vertical angles congruent?

Fill in the conjecture using your work in this investigation.

> **Vertical Angles Conjecture** If two angles are vertical angles, then they    **C-2**
> are _____.

You used inductive reasoning to discover the Linear Pair Conjecture and the Vertical Angles Conjecture. The example in your book shows that, if you accept that the Linear Pair Conjecture is true, you can use deductive reasoning to show that the Vertical Angles Conjecture must also be true. Read the example very carefully and make sure you understand each step of the deductive argument.

(continued)

Here is another example to help you write deductive arguments.

**EXAMPLE**  **a.** Use inductive reasoning to complete this conjecture.

If $\angle B$ is the supplement of an acute angle $A$ and $\angle C$ is the complement of $\angle A$, then $m\angle B - m\angle C =$ _____.

**b.** Write a deductive argument to show why the conjecture is true.

▶ **Solution**  **a.** The diagrams below show three examples.

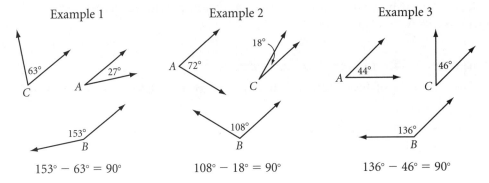

In each case, $m\angle B - m\angle C = 90°$. Based on these examples, the conjecture would be

If $\angle B$ is the supplement of an acute angle $A$ and $\angle C$ is the complement of $\angle A$, then $m\angle B - m\angle C = 90°$.

**Deductive Argument:** The measures of supplementary angles add up to 180°.

$$m\angle A + m\angle B = 180°$$

The measures of complementary angles add up to 90°.

$$m\angle A + m\angle C = 90°$$

Solve the second equation for $m\angle A$.

$$m\angle A = 90° - m\angle C$$

Substitute $90° - m\angle C$ for $m\angle A$ in the first equation.

$$90° - m\angle C + m\angle B = 180°$$

Subtract 90° from both sides of the equation.

$$-m\angle C + m\angle B = 90°$$

Rewrite the left side of the equation to complete the deductive argument.

$$m\angle B - m\angle C = 90°$$

The Vertical Angles Conjecture states that *if* two angles are vertical angles, *then* they are congruent. When you reverse the "if" and "then" parts of an "if-then" statement, you get the **converse** of the statement. Here is the converse of the Vertical Angles Conjecture.

*If* two angles are congruent, *then* they are vertical angles.

Is this statement true? The diagram on page 124 of your book shows a *counterexample* to this statement. If you can find even one counterexample, then the statement is false. So, the converse of the Vertical Angles Conjecture is false.

# 2.6 Special Angles on Parallel Lines

In this lesson you will

- Make three conjectures about the angles formed when two parallel lines are intersected by a **transversal**
- Determine whether the converse of each conjecture is true
- Prove one of the conjectures assuming one of the other conjectures is true

A line that intersects two or more coplanar lines is called a **transversal.** In your book, read about the three types of angle pairs formed when a transversal intersects two lines. In the investigation you will look at the angles formed when a transversal intersects two *parallel* lines.

## Investigation 1: Which Angles Are Congruent?

Follow the instructions before Step 1 to create parallel lines $k$ and $\ell$ intersected by transversal $m$. Number the angles as shown.

Place a piece of patty paper over the set of angles 1, 2, 3, and 4. Copy the two intersecting lines $m$ and $k$ and the four angles onto the patty paper.

Angles 1 and 5 are corresponding angles. Place the tracing of ∠1 over ∠5. How do the angles compare? Repeat this process for the other pairs of corresponding angles (∠3 and ∠7, ∠2 and ∠6, ∠4 and ∠8). Use your findings to complete this conjecture.

> **Corresponding Angles Conjecture, or CA Conjecture** If two parallel lines are cut by a transversal, then corresponding angles are _____. **C-3a**

Angles 3 and 6 are alternate interior angles. Place the tracing of ∠3 over ∠6. How do the angles compare? Repeat this process for the other pair of alternate interior angles (∠4 and ∠5), and then complete this conjecture.

> **Alternate Interior Angles Conjecture, or AIA Conjecture** If two parallel lines are cut by a transversal, then alternate interior angles are _____. **C-3b**

Angles 1 and 8 are alternate exterior angles. Place the tracing of ∠1 over ∠8. How do the angles compare? Repeat this process for the other pair of alternate exterior angles (∠2 and ∠7), and then complete this conjecture.

> **Alternate Exterior Angles Conjecture, or AEA Conjecture** If two parallel lines are cut by a transversal, then alternate exterior angles are _____. **C-3c**

The three conjectures above can be combined to create the Parallel Lines Conjecture.

> **Parallel Lines Conjecture** If two parallel lines are cut by a transversal, then corresponding angles are _____, alternate interior angles are _____, and alternate exterior angles are _____. **C-3**

(continued)

Now draw two lines that are *not* parallel and a transversal cutting both lines. Use the same process you used above to compare corresponding angles, alternate interior angles, and alternate exterior angles. Do the conjectures work for nonparallel lines?

## Investigation 2: Is the Converse True?

In this investigation you'll consider the converse of the Corresponding Angles Conjecture: If two lines are cut by a transversal to form a pair of congruent corresponding angles, then the lines are parallel. Do you think this statement is true? Investigate by following Step 1 in your book.

Now write the converse of each of the other two conjectures. Do you think the converses are true? Investigate by following Step 2 in your book. Then complete the following conjecture.

**Converse of the Parallel Lines Conjecture** If two lines are cut by a transversal to form a pair of congruent corresponding angles, congruent alternate interior angles, or congruent alternate exterior angles, then the lines are _____.

C-4

If you accept any of the three parallel lines conjectures as true, you can use deductive reasoning (and possibly some earlier conjectures) to show that the others are true. The example in your book shows that if you accept the Corresponding Angles and Vertical Angles Conjectures as true, then you can prove that the Alternate Interior Angles Conjecture is true. Read the example carefully. Here is another example.

**EXAMPLE** | Suppose you assume that the Alternate Interior Angles Conjecture is true. Write a deductive argument showing that the Alternate Exterior Angles Conjecture must be true. (You may assume that the Vertical Angles Conjecture is true.)

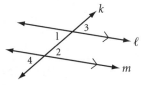

**Solution** | **Deductive Argument:** In the diagram, lines $\ell$ and $m$ are parallel and intersected by transversal $k$. Because we assume that the alternate interior angles are congruent

$$m\angle 1 = m\angle 2$$

Because we assume the Vertical Angles Conjecture is true

$$m\angle 1 = m\angle 3 \text{ and } m\angle 2 = m\angle 4$$

Substitute $m\angle 3$ for $m\angle 1$ and $m\angle 4$ for $m\angle 2$ in the first equation.

$$m\angle 3 = m\angle 4$$

So, the alternate exterior angles, $\angle 3$ and $\angle 4$, are congruent.

Therefore, if the alternate interior angles are congruent, then the alternate exterior angles are also congruent.

## CONDENSED
## LESSON
# 3.1 Duplicating Segments and Angles

In this lesson you will

- Learn what it means to create a **geometric construction**
- **Duplicate a segment** by using a straightedge and a compass and by using patty paper and a straightedge
- **Duplicate an angle** by using a straightedge and a compass and by using patty paper and a straightedge

In geometry, there are several methods for creating a figure.

- You can *sketch* a figure without using geometry tools. Make a sketch when exact measurements are not important.
- You can *draw* a figure using measuring tools, such as a protractor and a ruler. Make a drawing when it is important for lengths and angle measures to be precise.
- You can *construct* a figure using a compass and straightedge. When you make a construction, do *not* use your measuring tools. Compass-and-straightedge constructions allow you to accurately draw congruent segments and angles, segment and angle bisectors, and parallel and perpendicular lines.
- You can also *construct* a figure using patty paper and a straightedge. As with compass-and-straightedge constructions, patty-paper constructions do not use measuring tools.

In this lesson you will focus on constructions. You can read about the history of constructions in the lesson introduction in your book.

### Investigation 1: Duplicating a Segment

In this investigation you will copy this segment using only a compass and straightedge. This is called *duplicating* a segment. When you construct a figure, you may use a ruler as a straightedge, but *not* as a measuring tool.

Draw a ray on your paper that extends longer than $\overline{AB}$. Label the endpoint of the ray point *C*. Now think about how you can use *only* your compass to create a segment, $\overline{CD}$, that is the same length as $\overline{AB}$. Try constructing $\overline{CD}$ on your own before looking at Step 1 of the investigation in your book. You can use a ruler to check that $\overline{AB} \cong \overline{CD}$.

Step 1 shows the three stages involved in duplicating segment *AB*. The stages are described below.

**Stage 1:** Draw a ray that extends longer than $\overline{AB}$ and label the endpoint *C*.

**Stage 2:** Put the sharp end of your compass on point *A*. Open the compass until the other end touches point *B*, and make an arc.

**Stage 3:** *Without changing the opening of your compass*, put the sharp end of your compass on point *C* and make an arc on the ray. Label the point where the arc intersects the ray point *D*. Segment *CD* is congruent to segment *AB*.

(continued)

## Lesson 3.1 • Duplicating Segments and Angles (continued)

To duplicate $\overline{AB}$ using patty paper, simply place the patty paper over the segment and trace it, using a straightedge to ensure the tracing is straight.

### Investigation 2: Duplicating an Angle

In this investigation you will copy this angle using a compass and straightedge.

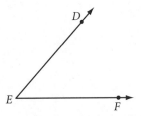

Draw a ray that extends longer than a side of $\angle DEF$. Label the endpoint of the ray G. This ray will be one side of the duplicate angle. Try to figure out how to duplicate $\angle DEF$ on your own before looking at Step 1 in your book. You can use a protractor to check that the angles are congruent.

Step 1 shows the first two stages involved in duplicating $\angle DEF$. The stages are described below.

**Stage 1:** Use your compass to construct an arc with its center at point E. The arc should intersect both sides of the angle. *Without changing the opening of your compass,* make an arc centered at point G.

**Stage 2:** On $\angle DEF$, put the sharp end of your compass on the point where the arc intersects $\overrightarrow{EF}$. Adjust the opening so that the other end touches the point where the arc intersects $\overrightarrow{ED}$, and make an arc. *Without changing the opening of your compass,* put the sharp end of your compass on the point where the arc intersects the ray with endpoint G, and make an arc that intersects the original arc.

To finish the construction, draw a ray from point G through the point where the two arcs intersect. Use a protractor to verify that $\angle G$ is congruent to $\angle DEF$.

Practice duplicating other angles until you are sure you understand the steps. Be sure to try duplicating obtuse angles as well as acute angles.

Now try to duplicate $\angle DEF$ using patty paper instead of a compass.

Write a summary of the construction methods you learned in this lesson.

# Constructing Perpendicular Bisectors

In this lesson you will

- Construct the **perpendicular bisector** of a segment using patty paper and a straightedge, and using a compass and straightedge
- Complete the **Perpendicular Bisector Conjecture**
- Learn about **medians** and **midsegments** of triangles

A **segment bisector** is a line, ray, or segment that passes through the midpoint of the segment. A line that passes through the midpoint of a segment and that is perpendicular to the segment is the **perpendicular bisector** of the segment. A segment has an infinite number of bisectors, but in a plane it has *only one* perpendicular bisector.

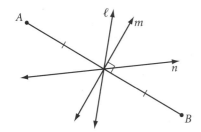

Lines ℓ, *m*, and *n* bisect $\overline{AB}$.
Line *m* is the perpendicular bisector of $\overline{AB}$.

## Investigation 1: Finding the Right Bisector

Follow Steps 1–3 in your book to construct a perpendicular bisector of $\overline{PQ}$ using patty paper.

Place three points—*A*, *B*, and *C*—on the perpendicular bisector, and use your compass to compare the distances *PA* and *QA*, *PB* and *QB*, and *PC* and *QC*. In each case, you should find that the distances are equal. These findings lead to the following conjecture.

> **Perpendicular Bisector Conjecture** If a point is on the perpendicular bisector of a segment, then it is equidistant from the endpoints.

C-5

Is the converse of this statement also true? That is, if a point is equidistant from the endpoints of a segment, is it on the segment's perpendicular bisector? If the converse is true, then locating two such points can help you locate the perpendicular bisector.

## Investigation 2: Right Down the Middle

In this investigation you will use a compass and straightedge to construct the perpendicular bisector of a segment. First, draw a line segment. Then follow the steps below.

Adjust your compass so that the opening is more than half the length of the segment. Using one endpoint as the center, make an arc on one side of the segment.

(continued)

*Without changing the opening of your compass,* put the sharp end of your compass on the other endpoint and make an arc intersecting the first arc.

The point where the arcs intersect is equidistant from the two endpoints. Follow the same steps to locate another such point on the other side of the segment. Then draw a line through the two points.

The line you drew is the perpendicular bisector of the segment. You can check this by folding the segment so that the endpoints coincide (as you did in Investigation 1). The line should fall on the crease of the paper.

The construction you did in this investigation demonstrates the conjecture below.

**Converse of the Perpendicular Bisector Conjecture** If a point is equidistant from the endpoints of a segment, then it is on the perpendicular bisector of the segment.

**C-6**

Now that you know how to construct a perpendicular bisector, you can locate the midpoint of any segment. This allows you to construct two special types of segments related to triangles: medians and midsegments.

A **median** is a segment that connects a vertex of a triangle to the midpoint of the opposite side. To construct the median from vertex $B$, use the perpendicular bisector construction to locate the midpoint of $\overline{AC}$. Then connect vertex $B$ to this point.

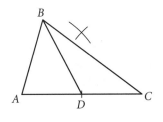

A **midsegment** is a segment that connects the midpoints of two sides of a triangle. To construct a midsegment from $\overline{PR}$ to $\overline{QR}$, use the perpendicular bisector construction two times to locate midpoints of $\overline{PR}$ and $\overline{QR}$. Then connect the midpoints.

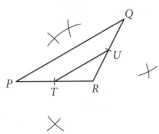

Write a summary of the construction methods you learned in this lesson.

# Constructing Perpendiculars to a Line

In this lesson you will

- Construct the **perpendicular** to a line from a point not on the line
- Complete the **Shortest Distance Conjecture**
- Learn about **altitudes** of triangles

In Lesson 3.2, you learned to construct the perpendicular bisector of a segment. In this lesson you will use what you learned to construct the perpendicular to a line from a point not on the line.

## Investigation 1: Finding the Right Line

Draw a line and a point labeled *P* that is not on the line. With the sharp end of your compass at point *P*, make two arcs on the line. Label the intersection points *A* and *B*.

Note that *PA* = *PB*, so point *P* is on the perpendicular bisector of $\overline{AB}$. Use the construction you learned in Lesson 3.2 to construct the perpendicular bisector of $\overline{AB}$. Label the midpoint of $\overline{AB}$ point *M*. You have now constructed a perpendicular to a line from a point not on the line. Now choose any three points on $\overleftrightarrow{AB}$ and label them *Q*, *R*, and *S*. Measure *PQ*, *PR*, *PS*, and *PM*. Which distance is shortest?

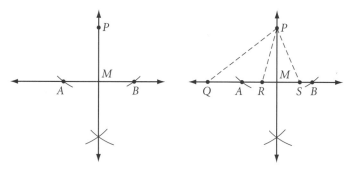

Your observations should lead to this conjecture.

---

**Shortest Distance Conjecture** The shortest distance from a point to a line is measured along the perpendicular segment from the point to the line.     `C-7`

---

In the next investigation you will use patty paper to create a perpendicular from a point to a line.

(continued)

### Investigation 2: Patty-Paper Perpendiculars

On a piece of patty paper, draw a line $\overleftrightarrow{AB}$ and a point $P$ that is not on $\overleftrightarrow{AB}$.

Fold the line onto itself. Slide the layers of paper (keeping $\overleftrightarrow{AB}$ aligned with itself) until point $P$ is on the fold.

Crease the paper, open it up, and draw a line on the crease. The line is the perpendicular to $\overleftrightarrow{AB}$ through point $P$. (Why?)

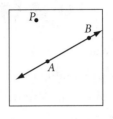
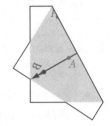

Step 1          Step 2

Constructing a perpendicular from a point to a line allows you to find the distance from the point to the line, which is defined as follows, "The **distance from a point to a line** is the length of the perpendicular segment from the point to the line."

The **altitude** of a triangle is a perpendicular segment from a vertex of a triangle to the line containing the opposite side. The length of this segment is the height of the triangle. The illustrations on page 156 of your book show that an altitude can be inside or outside the triangle, or it can be one of the triangle's sides. A triangle has three different altitudes, so it has three different heights.

**EXAMPLE** | Construct the altitude from vertex $A$ of $\triangle ABC$.

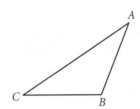

▶ **Solution** | Extend $\overline{CB}$ to become $\overleftrightarrow{CB}$ and construct a perpendicular segment from point $A$ to $\overleftrightarrow{CB}$.

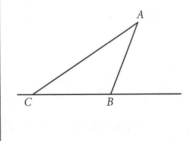
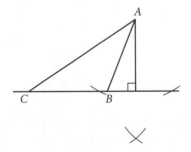

Write a summary of the construction methods you learned in this lesson.

*Discovering Geometry Condensed Lessons*
©2008 Key Curriculum Press

# Constructing Angle Bisectors

In this lesson you will

- Construct an **angle bisector** using patty paper and a straightedge, and using a compass and a straightedge
- Complete the **Angle Bisector Conjecture**

An **angle bisector** is a ray that divides an angle into two congruent angles. You can also refer to a segment as an angle bisector if the segment lies on the ray and passes through the angle vertex.

## Investigation 1: Angle Bisecting by Folding

Follow Steps 1–3 in your book to construct the bisector of acute ∠*PQR* using patty paper. You can tell the ray you construct is the angle bisector because the fold forms two angles that coincide.

Now construct the bisector of an obtuse angle. Can you use the same method you used to bisect the acute angle?

Does every angle have a bisector? Is it possible for an angle to have more than one bisector? If you are not sure, experiment until you think you know the answers to both of these questions.

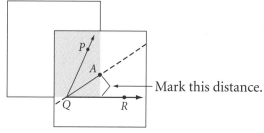

Mark this distance.

Look at the angles you bisected. Do you see a relationship between the points on the angle bisector and the sides of the angle? Choose one of the bisected angles. Choose any point on the bisector and label it *A*. Compare the distances from *A* to each of the two sides. (Remember that "distance" means *shortest* distance.) To do this, you can place one edge of a second piece of patty paper on one side of the angle. Slide the edge of the patty paper along the side of the angle until an adjacent perpendicular side of the patty paper passes through the point. Mark this distance on the patty paper.

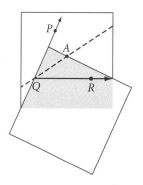

Compare this distance with the distance to the other side of the angle by repeating the process on the other ray.

Your observations should lead to this conjecture.

---

**Angle Bisector Conjecture** If a point is on the bisector of an angle, then it is equidistant from the sides of the angle.  **C-8**

---

(continued)

### Investigation 2: Angle Bisecting with Compass

You can also construct an angle bisector using a compass and straightedge.

Draw an angle. To start the construction, draw an arc centered at the vertex of the angle that crosses both sides of the angle.

Try to complete the construction on your own before reading the following text. Don't be afraid to experiment. If you make a mistake, you can always start over. When you think you have constructed an angle bisector, fold your paper to check whether the ray you constructed is actually the bisector.

*Constructing the angle bisector:* Place the sharp end of your compass on one of the points where the arc intersects the angle, and make an arc. *Without changing the opening of your compass,* repeat this process with the other point of intersection. If the two small arcs do not intersect, make your compass opening larger and repeat the last two steps. Draw the ray from the vertex of the angle to the point where the two small arcs intersect.

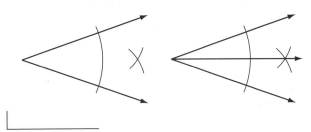

**EXAMPLE** | Construct an angle with a measure of exactly 45° using only a compass and straightedge.

▶ **Solution** | Construct a 90° angle by constructing the perpendicular to a line from a point not on the line. (Look back at Lesson 3.3 if you need to review this construction.) Then use the angle-bisector construction you learned in this lesson to bisect the 90° angle.

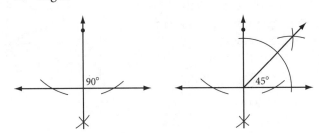

Write a summary of the construction methods you learned in this lesson.

# 3.5 Constructing Parallel Lines

In this lesson you will

- Construct **parallel lines** using patty paper and a straightedge

As you learned in Chapter 1, **parallel lines** are lines that lie in the same plane and do not intersect. So, any two points on one parallel line will be equidistant from the other line. You can use this idea to construct a line parallel to a given line.

## Investigation: Constructing Parallel Lines by Folding

Follow Steps 1–3 in your book to construct parallel lines with patty paper. Notice that the pairs of corresponding angles, alternate interior angles, and alternate exterior angles are congruent. (In this case, all are pairs of right angles.)

The next example shows another way to construct parallel lines.

**EXAMPLE** | Use the Converse of the Alternate Interior Angles Conjecture to construct a pair of parallel lines. (Try to do this on your own before reading the solution.)

▶ **Solution** | Draw two intersecting lines and label them *m* and *n*. Label their point of intersection *P* and label one of the angles formed ∠1. On line *n*, label a point *Q* that is on the same side of line *m* as ∠1. Using point *Q* as the vertex and $\overrightarrow{QP}$ as a side, duplicate ∠1 on the opposite side of line *n*. Label the new angle ∠2. Extend the side of ∠2 into line *q*.

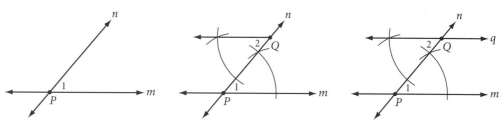

Notice that line *m* and line *q* are cut by a transversal (line *n*) to form a congruent pair of alternate interior angles (∠1 and ∠2). According to the converse of the AIA Conjecture, *m* ∥ *q*.

Now see if you can use the Converse of the Corresponding Angles Conjecture or the Converse of the Alternate Exterior Angles Conjecture to construct a pair of parallel lines.

Write a summary of the construction methods you learned in this lesson.

# 3.6 Construction Problems

In this lesson you will

- Construct polygons given information about some of the sides and angles

In this chapter you have learned to construct congruent segments and angles, angle and segment bisectors, perpendiculars, perpendicular bisectors, and parallel lines. Once you know these basic constructions, you can create more advanced geometric figures.

Example A in your book shows you how to construct a triangle if you are given three segments to use as sides. This example also explores an important question: If you are given three segments, how many different-size triangles can you form? Read the example carefully.

Example B shows you how to construct a triangle if you are given three angles. This example shows that three angles do *not* determine a unique triangle. Given three angle measures, you can draw an infinite number of triangles. The triangles will all have the same shape, but they will be different sizes.

The examples below show some other constructions.

**EXAMPLE A** | Use a compass and a straightedge to construct $\triangle PQR$ with $\overline{PQ}$ as a side, and with $m\angle P = 90°$ and $m\angle Q = 45°$.

▶ **Solution** | To construct $\angle P$, extend $\overline{PQ}$ to the left and construct a perpendicular to $\overleftrightarrow{PQ}$ through point $P$. To construct $\angle Q$, first construct a perpendicular to $\overleftrightarrow{PQ}$ through point $Q$. This creates a right angle with vertex $Q$. To create a 45° angle, bisect this angle.

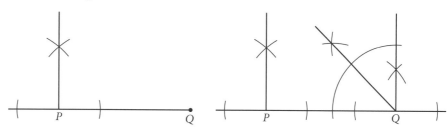

To complete the construction, extend the sides of $\angle P$ and $\angle Q$ until they intersect. Label the intersection point $R$.

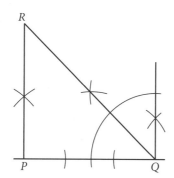

(continued)

**EXAMPLE B**  | Construct kite *KITE* with *KI* = *KE* and *TI* = *TE*, using the segments and angle below.

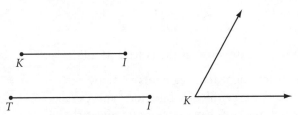

▸ **Solution** | Duplicate $\overline{KI}$ and ∠*K*. Because *KI* = *KE*, duplicate $\overline{KI}$ on the other side of ∠*K* to create side $\overline{KE}$.

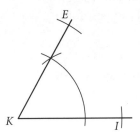

To locate vertex *T*, make a large arc with radius *TI* centered at point *I*. Vertex *T* must be on this arc. Because *TI* = *TE*, draw another large arc with radius *TI* centered at point *E*. The intersection of the two arcs is point *T*. Connect points *E* and *I* to point *T* to complete the kite.

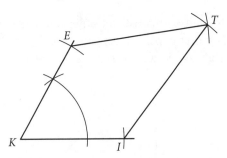

# Constructing Points of Concurrency

In this lesson you will

- Construct the **incenter, circumcenter,** and **orthocenter** of a triangle
- Make conjectures about the properties of the incenter and circumcenter of a triangle
- **Circumscribe** a circle about a triangle and **inscribe** a circle in a triangle

You can use the constructions you learned in this chapter to construct special segments related to triangles. In this lesson you will construct the angle bisectors and altitudes of a triangle, and the perpendicular bisectors of a triangle's sides. After you construct each set of three segments, you will determine whether they are *concurrent*. Three or more segments, lines, rays, or planes are **concurrent** if they intersect in a single point. The point of intersection is called the **point of concurrency.**

## Investigation 1: Concurrence

You can perform the constructions in this investigation with patty paper and a straightedge or with a compass and straightedge. Save your constructions to use in Investigation 2.

If you are using patty paper, draw a large acute triangle on one sheet and a large obtuse triangle on another. If you are using a compass, draw the triangles on the top and bottom halves of a piece of paper.

Construct the three angle bisectors of each triangle. You should find that they are concurrent. The point of concurrency is called the **incenter** of the triangle.

Start with two new triangles, one acute and one obtuse, and construct the perpendicular bisector of each side. You should find that, in each triangle, the three perpendicular bisectors are concurrent. The point of concurrency is called the **circumcenter.**

Finally, start with two new triangles and construct the altitude to each side. These segments are also concurrent. The point of concurrency is called the **orthocenter.**

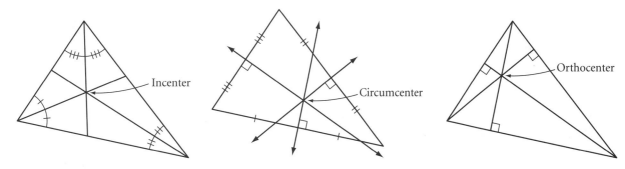

Your observations in this investigation lead to the following conjectures.

**Angle Bisector Concurrency Conjecture** The three angle bisectors of a triangle are concurrent.

`C-9`

(continued)

> **Perpendicular Bisector Concurrency Conjecture** The three perpendicular bisectors of a triangle are concurrent. **C-10**

> **Altitude Concurrency Conjecture** The three altitudes (or the lines containing the altitudes) of a triangle are concurrent. **C-11**

For what type of triangle will the incenter, circumcenter, and orthocenter be the same point? If you don't know, experiment with different types of triangles (scalene, isosceles, equilateral, acute, obtuse, right).

## Investigation 2: Circumcenter

For this investigation you will need your triangles from Investigation 1 that show the perpendicular bisectors of the sides. For each triangle, measure the distance from the circumcenter to each of the three vertices. Are the distances the same? Now measure the distance from the circumcenter to each of the three sides. Are the distances the same? Use a compass to construct a circle with the circumcenter as center that passes through a vertex of the triangle. What do you notice?

You can state your findings as the Circumcenter Conjecture.

> **Circumcenter Conjecture** The circumcenter of a triangle is equidistant from the three vertices. **C-12**

## Investigation 3: Incenter

You will need your triangles from Investigation 1 that show the angle bisectors. For each triangle, measure the distance from the incenter to each of the three vertices. Are the distances the same?

Construct the perpendicular from the incenter to any one of the sides of the triangle. Mark the point of intersection between the perpendicular and the side. Now use a compass to construct a circle with the incenter as center that passes through the point you just marked. What do you notice? What can you conclude about the distance of the incenter from each of the sides?

You can state your findings as the Incenter Conjecture.

> **Incenter Conjecture** The incenter of a triangle is equidistant from the three sides. **C-13**

Read the deductive argument for the Circumcenter Conjecture on pages 180–181 of your book and make sure you understand it.

A circle that passes through each vertex of a polygon is **circumscribed** about the polygon. The polygon is **inscribed** in the circle.

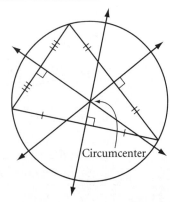

Circumcenter

(continued)

A circle that is tangent to each side of a polygon is **inscribed** in the polygon. The polygon is **circumscribed** about the circle.

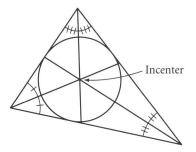

Why does the method for constructing the circumcenter guarantee that it is the center of the circle that is circumscribed about the triangle? Write down your own reasons before you read the logical argument below. You might use the diagram to help you write your argument.

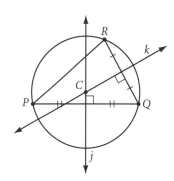

### Deductive Argument

A circle is the set of points equidistant from a center point. If a point is located equidistant from the three vertices of a triangle, that point can be used as the center of a circle circumscribed about the triangle.

If the Perpendicular Bisector Conjecture is true, every point on the perpendicular bisector of a segment is equidistant from the two endpoints. So every point on line $k$ is equidistant from points $R$ and $Q$, and every point on line $j$ is equidistant from points $P$ and $Q$. Because circumcenter $C$ lies at the intersection of lines $j$ and $k$, point $C$ must be equidistant from all three vertices, points $R$, $Q$, and $P$. If a circle is constructed with center $C$ that passes through one vertex, for example, point $R$, it will also pass through the other two because all points on a circle lie the same distance from the center. That circle is the circumscribed circle about $\triangle PQR$.

Use a similar logical argument to explain why the incenter is the center of the inscribed circle. Write down your own logical argument before you read the one on the next page. Use the diagram to help you.

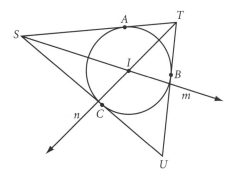

(continued)

### Deductive Argument

A circle is the set of points equidistant from a given center point. If a point is equidistant from the three sides of a triangle, it can be used as the center for an inscribed circle.

If the Angle Bisector Conjecture is true, every point on the angle bisector is equidistant from the two sides of the angle. Therefore, in △STU each point on angle bisector $m$ is equidistant from triangle sides $\overline{ST}$ and $\overline{SU}$. Similarly, each point on angle bisector $n$ is equidistant from triangle sides $\overline{ST}$ and $\overline{TU}$. Because incenter $I$ lies on both angle bisectors $m$ and $n$, it is equidistant from all three sides. Thus, the circle with center at incenter $I$ that is tangent to one of the sides will also be tangent to the other two sides. That circle is the inscribed circle in the triangle.

**EXAMPLE** | Inscribe a circle in △QRS.

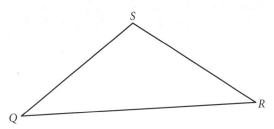

▶ **Solution** | To find the center of the circle, construct the incenter. Note that you need to construct only two angle bisectors to locate the incenter. (Why?)

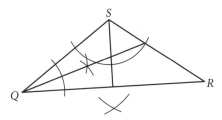

The radius of the circle is the distance from the incenter to each side. To find the radius, construct a perpendicular from the incenter to one of the sides. Here, we construct the perpendicular to $\overline{RS}$. Now, draw the circle.

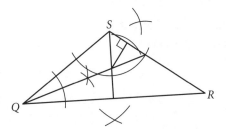 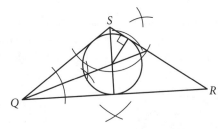

# The Centroid

In this lesson you will

- Construct the **centroid** of a triangle
- Make conjectures about the properties of the centroid of a triangle

You have seen that the three angle bisectors, the three perpendicular bisectors of the sides, and the three altitudes of a triangle are concurrent. In this lesson you will look at the three medians of a triangle.

## Investigation 1: Are Medians Concurrent?

On a sheet of patty paper, draw a large scalene acute triangle and label it *CNR*. Locate the midpoints of the three sides and construct the medians. You should find that the medians are concurrent. Save this triangle.

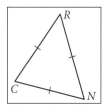 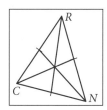

Now start with a scalene obtuse triangle and construct the three medians. Are the medians concurrent? You can state your findings as a conjecture.

> **Median Concurrency Conjecture** The three medians of a triangle are concurrent.    `C-14`

The point of concurrency of the three medians is the **centroid.** On your acute triangle, label the medians $\overline{CT}$, $\overline{NO}$, and $\overline{RE}$. Label the centroid *D*.

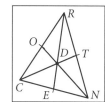

Use your compass or patty paper to investigate the centroid: Is the centroid equidistant from the three vertices? Is it equidistant from the three sides? Is the centroid the midpoint of each median?

The centroid *D* divides each median into two segments. For each median, find the ratio of the length of the longer segment to the length of the shorter segment. You should find that, for each median, the ratio is the same. Use your findings to complete this conjecture.

> **Centroid Conjecture** The centroid of a triangle divides each median into    `C-15`
> two parts so that the distance from the centroid to the vertex is _____
> the distance from the centroid to the midpoint of the opposite side.

In Lesson 3.7, you learned that the circumcenter of a triangle is the center of the circumscribed circle and the incenter is the center of the inscribed circle. In the next investigation you will discover a special property of the centroid.

*(continued)*

### Investigation 2: Balancing Act

For this investigation you will need a sheet of cardboard and your scalene acute triangle from Investigation 1.

Place your patty-paper triangle on the cardboard. With your compass point, mark the three vertices, the three midpoints, and the centroid on the cardboard. Remove the patty paper and carefully draw the triangle and the medians on the cardboard. Cut out the cardboard triangle.

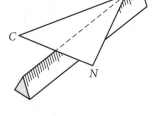

Try balancing the triangle by placing one of its medians on the edge of a ruler.

You should be able to get the triangle to balance. Repeat the process with each of the other medians. The fact that you can balance the triangle on each median means that each median divides the triangle into two triangular regions of equal area.

Now try to balance the triangle by placing its centroid on the end of a pencil or pen. If you have traced and cut out the triangle carefully, it should balance. Because the triangle balances on its centroid, the centroid is the triangle's **center of gravity.**

You can state your findings as a conjecture.

**Center of Gravity Conjecture** The centroid of a triangle is the center of gravity of the triangular region.

**C-16**

Notice that it makes sense that the triangle balances on the centroid because it balances on each median, and the centroid is on each median. As long as the weight of the cardboard is distributed evenly throughout the triangle, you can balance any triangle on its centroid.

*Discovering Geometry Condensed Lessons*
©2008 Key Curriculum Press

# 4.1 Triangle Sum Conjecture

In this lesson you will

- State a conjecture about the sum of the measures of the angles in a triangle
- Complete a paragraph proof of the **Triangle Sum Conjecture**

In this chapter you will focus on properties of triangles. To start, you will look at the angle measures of triangles.

## Investigation: The Triangle Sum

Draw two large acute triangles with very different shapes and two large obtuse triangles with very different shapes.

For each triangle, measure the three angles as accurately as possible, and then find the sum of the three measures. You should find that the angle sum for each triangle is the same. What is the angle sum?

To check this sum, write the letters *a, b,* and *c* in the interiors of the three angles of one of the acute triangles, and carefully cut out the triangle. Then tear off the three angles of the triangle and arrange them so that their vertices meet at a point.

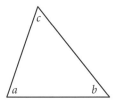 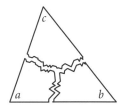 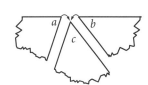

How does the arrangement verify the angle sum you found above?

Your work in this investigation leads to the following conjecture.

> **Triangle Sum Conjecture** The sum of the measures of the angles in every triangle is 180°.    **C-17**

Next you will write a **paragraph proof** to show why the Triangle Sum Conjecture is true. In your proof, you can use conjectures, definitions, and properties to support your argument. Look at the figure at right. △*ABC* is any triangle. $\overleftrightarrow{EC}$ is drawn parallel to $\overline{AB}$. *Note:* $\overleftrightarrow{EC}$ is an **auxiliary line** (or helping line) because it is an extra line added to the figure to help with the proof. Consider the questions on page 201 of your book.

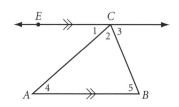

Copy the diagram and mark angle relationships that might help with your proof. Then use the diagram and your answers to these questions to write a paragraph proof explaining why the Triangle Sum Conjecture is true.

After you have finished, compare your paragraph proof with the one on page 202 of your book.

(continued)

The Triangle Sum Conjecture allows you to construct the third angle of a triangle if you are given two of the angles. Work through the example in your book. The following example shows a slightly different method. Try it to see whether one method is easier. Can you find another method that works?

**EXAMPLE A** | Given ∠P and ∠Q of △PQR, construct ∠R.

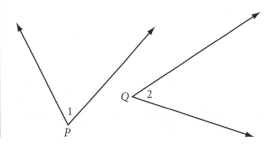

▶ **Solution** | Draw a line and construct ∠P opening to the right on this line. Construct ∠Q so that it shares both the vertex of ∠P and the side of ∠P that is not on the line. The angle labeled 3 on the diagram is ∠R, because the sum of the measures of the three angles is 180°.

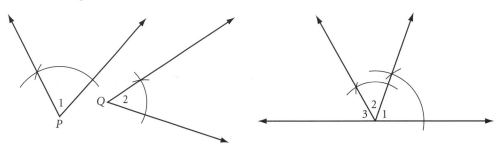

The following example applies what you have learned in this lesson.

**EXAMPLE B** | Find the lettered angle measures.

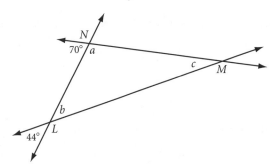

▶ **Solution** | The angle labeled *a* and the 70° angle form a linear pair, so *a* + 70° = 180°. Therefore, *a* = 110°. The angle labeled *b* and the 44° angle are vertical angles, so *b* = 44°. By the Triangle Sum Conjecture, 110° + 44° + *c* = 180°, so *c* = 26°.

# CONDENSED
## LESSON
## 4.2    Properties of Isosceles Triangles

In this lesson you will

- Discover how the angles of an isosceles triangle are related
- Make a conjecture about triangles that have two congruent angles

An *isosceles triangle* is a triangle with at least two congruent sides. The angle between the congruent sides is called the *vertex angle*. The other two angles are called the *base angles*. The side between the base angles is called the *base*. The other two sides are called the *legs*.

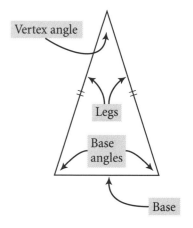

## Investigation 1: Base Angles in an Isosceles Triangle

Draw an acute angle $C$ on patty paper. Then follow Steps 2 and 3 in your book to construct an isosceles triangle, $\triangle ABC$.

Because $\overline{CA}$ and $\overline{CB}$ are the congruent sides, $\angle C$ is the vertex angle and $\angle A$ and $\angle B$ are base angles. Use your protractor to measure the base angles. How do the measures compare? Confirm your answer by folding your patty paper, keeping $\overline{AB}$ aligned with itself. Is $\angle A \cong \angle B$?

Now draw two more isosceles triangles, one with an obtuse vertex angle and one with a right vertex angle. Compare the base angles in each triangle. Are your findings the same as for the isosceles acute triangle?

Your observations should lead to the following conjecture.

> **Isosceles Triangle Conjecture** If a triangle is isosceles, then its base angles are congruent.    **C-18**

Equilateral triangles are also isosceles triangles, because at least two of their sides are congruent. How do you think the Isosceles Triangle Conjecture applies to equilateral triangles?

As you know, reversing the "if" and "then" parts of a conjecture gives the *converse* of the conjecture. Is the converse of the Isosceles Triangle Conjecture true? In other words, if a triangle has two congruent angles, is it isosceles? To test this statement, you need to draw a triangle with two congruent angles.

## Investigation 2: Is the Converse True?

Draw a segment, $\overline{AB}$, on your paper. Draw an acute angle at point $A$. In the finished triangle, $\angle A$ and $\angle B$ will be the congruent angles.

Notice that $\angle A$ must be acute. If it were right or obtuse, the sum of the measures of $\angle A$ and $\angle B$ would be greater than or equal to 180°, and, as you know, the sum of all *three* angle measures must be 180°.

(continued)

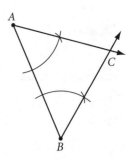

Now copy ∠A at point B on the same side of $\overline{AB}$. If necessary, extend the sides of the angles until they intersect. Label the point of intersection C.

Use your compass to compare the lengths of sides $\overline{AC}$ and $\overline{BC}$. Do they appear to be the same length? Check your answer using patty paper. Draw at least one more triangle with two congruent angles, and compare the side lengths. Your findings should provide evidence that the converse of the Isosceles Triangle Conjecture is true.

**Converse of the Isosceles Triangle Conjecture** If a triangle has two congruent angles, then it is an isosceles triangle.

**C-19**

The following example gives you practice applying what you have learned.

**EXAMPLE**

$m\angle A = $ _____

$m\angle D = $ _____

$EC = $ _____

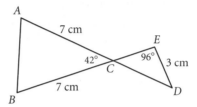

▶ **Solution**

By the Triangle Sum Conjecture, $m\angle A + m\angle B + 42° = 180°$, so $m\angle A + m\angle B = 138°$. Because ∠A and ∠B are the base angles of an isosceles triangle, they are congruent. So, $m\angle A = \frac{1}{2}(138°) = 69°$.

Because ∠ACB and ∠ECD are vertical angles, they are congruent. So, $m\angle ECD = 42°$. By the Triangle Sum Conjecture, $42° + 96° + m\angle D = 180°$. Solving for $m\angle D$ gives $m\angle D = 42°$.

Because $\angle ECD \cong \angle D$, $\triangle CDE$ is isosceles by the Converse of the Isosceles Triangle Conjecture. Therefore, the legs are congruent, so $EC = ED = 3$ cm.

*Discovering Geometry Condensed Lessons*
©2008 Key Curriculum Press

In this lesson you will

- Determine whether you can form a triangle from any three segments
- Discover a relationship between the side lengths and angle measures of a triangle
- Look for a relationship between the measure of the **exterior angle** of a triangle and the measures of the corresponding **remote interior angles**

If you are given three segments, will you always be able to form a triangle with those segments as sides? In the following investigation, you will explore this question.

## Investigation 1: What Is the Shortest Path from A to B?

In Step 1 of the investigation, you are given two sets of three segments to use as side lengths of triangles. Consider the first set of segments. To construct △CAT, first copy $\overline{CT}$. To construct the other two sides of the triangle, swing an arc of length AC centered at point C and an arc of length AT centered at point T. Point A is where the two arcs intersect.

Now try to use the second set of segments to construct △FSH. Are you able to do it? Why or why not?

You should have found that the arcs that you made using the lengths of two of the sides did not intersect, so it was not possible to construct △FSH. In general, for three segments to form a triangle, the sum of the lengths of any two segments must be greater than the length of the third segment. Here are two ways to visualize this.

Imagine two of the segments connected to the endpoints of the third segment by hinges. To form a triangle, you need to be able to swing the segments so that their unhinged endpoints meet but do not lie completely flat. This is possible only if the combined length of the two segments is greater than the length of the third segment.

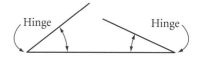

Imagine two segments connected by a hinge. To form a triangle, you need to be able to adjust the opening between these sides so that the unhinged endpoints meet the endpoints of the third segment, without lying completely flat. This is possible only if the combined length of the two hinged segments is greater than the length of the third segment.

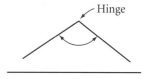

You can state this idea as a conjecture.

**Triangle Inequality Conjecture** The sum of the lengths of any two sides of    C-20
a triangle is greater than the length of the third side.

(continued)

You can think of the triangle conjecture in a different way: The shortest distance
between two points is along the segment connecting them. In other words, the
distance from $A$ to $C$ to $B$ cannot be shorter than the distance from $A$ to $B$.

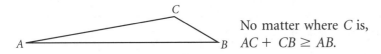

No matter where $C$ is,
$AC + CB \geq AB$.

## Investigation 2: Where Are the Largest and Smallest Angles?

Draw a scalene obtuse triangle. Follow Steps 1 and 2 in your book to label the
angles and sides according to their size. Then answer the questions in Step 3.

As in the example at right, you should find that the longest
side is opposite the angle with the largest measure, the
second longest side is opposite the side with the second
largest measure, and the shortest side is opposite the side
with the smallest measure.

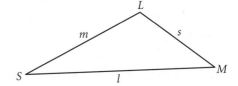

Draw a scalene acute triangle and follow Steps 1–3 again. Are your findings
the same?

State your findings as a conjecture. Here is one possible way to word
the conjecture.

**Side-Angle Inequality Conjecture** In a triangle, if one side is longer than
another side, then the angle opposite the longer side is larger than the angle
opposite the shorter side.   **C-21**

So far, you have been focusing on the *interior angles* of triangles.
Triangles also have *exterior angles*. To construct an **exterior angle,**
extend one side beyond the vertex. Each exterior angle of a triangle
has an **adjacent interior angle** and a pair of **remote interior angles.**

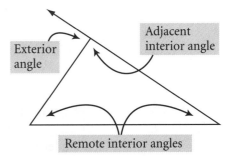

## Investigation 3: Exterior Angles of a Triangle

In this investigation you will look for a relationship between
the measure of an exterior angle and the measure of the two
associated remote interior angles. Follow Steps 1–3 in your
book for at least two different triangles. You can state your
findings as a conjecture.

**Triangle Exterior Angle Conjecture** The measure of an exterior angle of a   **C-22**
triangle is equal to the sum of the measures of the remote interior angles.

# Are There Congruence Shortcuts?

In this lesson you will

- Look for shortcuts for determining whether two triangles are congruent

If the three sides and three angles of one triangle are congruent to the three sides and three angles of another triangle, then you know the triangles are congruent. But, to determine whether two triangles are congruent, do you really need to make all six comparisons?

In this lesson and the next, you will search for shortcuts that allow you to determine whether two triangles are congruent by making only three comparisons. Page 221 of your book illustrates the six different ways that three parts of one triangle can be congruent to three parts of another. Note that the order in which the parts are listed is important. For example, Side-Angle-Side (SAS) refers to two sides and the angle included *between* the sides, while Side-Side-Angle (SSA) refers to two sides and an angle that is *not between* them.

## Investigation 1: Is SSS a Congruence Shortcut?

In this investigation you will explore the following question: If the three sides of one triangle are congruent to the three sides of another triangle, must the triangles be congruent? In other words, is Side-Side-Side (SSS) a congruence shortcut?

Follow Step 1 in your book to construct a triangle using the three given segments. Now try to construct a *different* triangle using the three segments as sides. Are you able to do it? (To determine whether two triangles are the same or different, you can place one on top of the other to see whether they coincide.)

You should find that you can make only one triangle from the three segments. In fact, if you are given *any* three segments (that satisfy the triangle inequality), you will be able to make only one triangle. That is, any two triangles with the same side lengths must be congruent. You can state this observation as a conjecture.

**SSS Congruence Conjecture** If the three sides of one triangle are congruent to the three sides of another triangle, then the triangles are congruent.

C-23

## Investigation 2: Is SAS a Congruence Shortcut?

Next you will consider the Side-Angle-Side (SAS) case. If two sides and the included angle of one triangle are congruent to two sides and the included angle of another, must the triangles be congruent?

Follow Step 1 in your book to construct a triangle from the three given parts. Now try to construct a *different* triangle from the same three parts. Are you able to do it? (Remember, the angle must be included *between* the sides.)

(continued)

You should find that you can make only one triangle from the given parts. In fact, if you are given *any* two sides and an included angle, you will be able to make only one triangle. You can state this observation as a conjecture.

> **SAS Congruence Conjecture** If two sides and the included angle of one triangle are congruent to two sides and the included angle of another triangle, then the triangles are congruent.
>
> **C-24**

## Investigation 3: Is SSA a Congruence Shortcut?

In this investigation you will explore the Side-Side-Angle (SSA) case. If two sides and a non-included angle of one triangle are congruent to the corresponding sides and angle of another triangle, must the triangles be congruent?

Follow Step 1 in your book to construct a triangle from the three given parts. Now try to construct a *different* triangle using the same two sides and non-included angle. Are you able to construct two different triangles using the same parts?

Point $U$ can be here or here.

Once you construct $\overline{ST}$ on a side of $\angle S$, there are two possible locations for point $U$ on the other side of the angle.

You can state this observation in a conjecture: If two sides and a non-included angle of one triangle are congruent to the corresponding two sides and non-included angle of another triangle, then the triangles are not necessarily congruent.

Here is an example that uses the new conjectures from this lesson.

**EXAMPLE** | Using *only* the information given, determine which triangles below are congruent and state which congruence shortcut you used.

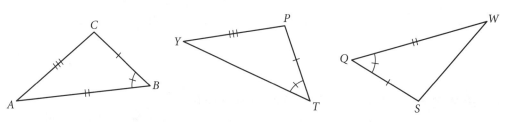

▶ **Solution** | Because $\overline{AB} \cong \overline{WQ}$, $\angle B \cong \angle Q$, and $\overline{BC} \cong \overline{QS}$, $\triangle ABC \cong \triangle WQS$ by SAS.

Although $\overline{BC} \cong \overline{TP}$, $\overline{PY} \cong \overline{CA}$, and $\angle B \cong \angle T$, you cannot conclude that $\triangle ABC \cong \triangle TPY$ because SSA is not a congruence shortcut.

For $\triangle TPY$ and $\triangle QSW$, you know only that $\angle Q \cong \angle T$ and $\overline{QS} \cong \overline{TP}$. This is not enough information to conclude that the triangles are congruent.

# Are There Other Congruence Shortcuts?

In this lesson you will

- Look for more shortcuts for determining whether two triangles are congruent

In Lesson 4.4, you saw that there are six ways in which three parts of one triangle can be congruent to three parts of another, and you investigated three of these cases. You learned the following congruence shortcuts.

- SSS: If three sides of one triangle are congruent to the three sides of another triangle, then the triangles are congruent.
- SAS: If two sides and the included angle of one triangle are congruent to two sides and the included angle of another triangle, then the triangles are congruent.

You also learned that if two sides and a non-included angle of one triangle are congruent to two sides and a non-included angle of another, then the triangles are *not* necessarily congruent. Now you will explore the three remaining cases.

A side that is between two given angles of a triangle is called an **included side**, as shown in the diagram at right.

Included side

## Investigation 1: Is ASA a Congruence Shortcut?

In this investigation you explore the Angle-Side-Angle (ASA) case. If two angles and the included side of one triangle are congruent to two angles and the included side of another, must the triangles be congruent?

Follow Step 1 in your book to construct a triangle using the three given parts. Now try to construct a *different* triangle using the three parts. Are you able to do it? (Remember, to determine whether two triangles are the same or different, you can place one on top of the other to see if they coincide.)

You should find that you can make only one triangle from the three given parts. In fact, if you are given any two angles and an included side, you will be able to make only one triangle. You can state this fact as a conjecture.

> **ASA Congruence Conjecture** If two angles and the included side of one triangle are congruent to two angles and the included side of another triangle, then the triangles are congruent. **C-25**

## Investigation 2: Is SAA a Triangle Congruence Shortcut?

Now consider Side-Angle-Angle (SAA), where the side is not included between the two angles.

Follow Step 1 in your book to construct a triangle from the three given parts. Now try to construct a *different* triangle using the same three parts. Are you able to do it?

**(continued)**

You should find that you can make only one triangle when given two angles and a non-included side. You can now state the following conjecture:

**SAA Congruence Conjecture** If two angles and a non-included side of one triangle are congruent to the corresponding angles and side of another triangle, then the triangles are congruent.

**C-26**

## Investigation 3: Is AAA a Triangle Congruence Shortcut?

Finally, you will explore the Angle-Angle-Angle (AAA) case. Construct a triangle from the three angles given in your book. Now try to construct a *different* triangle using the same three angles. Are you able to do it?

Because no side lengths are given, you can make the first side any length you like. By using a different length in your second triangle, you get a triangle of a different size.

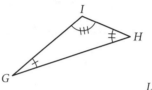 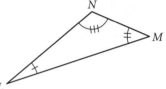

You can now state the following conjecture: If three angles of one triangle are congruent to the three angles of another triangle, then the two triangles are not necessarily congruent.

In the last two lessons, you have found that SSS, SAS, ASA, and SAA are all congruence shortcuts. Add them to your conjecture list. Here is an example.

**EXAMPLE** | Complete each statement and tell which congruence shortcut you used to determine that the triangles are congruent. If the triangles cannot be shown to be congruent, write "cannot be determined."

a. △ADB ≅ △ _____

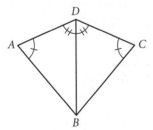

b. △STU ≅ △ _____

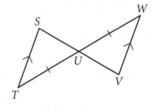

c. △EFX ≅ △ _____

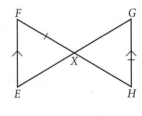

▶ **Solution** | a. Because ∠A ≅ ∠C, ∠ADB ≅ ∠CDB, and $\overline{BD} \cong \overline{BD}$, △ADB ≅ △CDB by SAA.

b. Because $\overline{ST}$ and $\overline{WV}$ are parallel, ∠S ≅ ∠V and ∠T ≅ ∠W. It is given that $\overline{TU} \cong \overline{WU}$. Therefore, △STU ≅ △VWU by SAA. You could also reason that ∠SUT ≅ ∠VUW because they are vertical angles, so △STU ≅ △VWU by ASA.

c. Cannot be determined. Because $\overline{EF}$ and $\overline{GH}$ are parallel, ∠E ≅ ∠G and ∠F ≅ ∠H. However, the congruent sides $\overline{FX}$ and $\overline{GH}$ are not corresponding. So, there is not enough information to show that the two triangles are congruent.

# Corresponding Parts of Congruent Triangles

In this lesson you will

- Use the fact that corresponding parts of congruent triangles are congruent to prove statements
- Learn techniques for keeping track of information when you are writing a proof

In Lessons 4.4 and 4.5, you discovered four shortcuts for showing that two triangles are congruent—SSS, SAS, ASA, and SAA. Once you have established that two triangles are congruent, you know that their corresponding parts are congruent. We will abbreviate the statement *corresponding parts of congruent triangles are congruent* as CPCTC.

Example A in your book uses CPCTC to prove that two segments are congruent. Read this example carefully. Notice that the argument first explains why the *triangles AMD* and *BMC* are congruent, and then uses CPCTC to explain why the *sides $\overline{AD}$* and *$\overline{BC}$* are congruent. Below is another example.

**EXAMPLE A**    Give a deductive argument to explain why $\overline{PT} \cong \overline{RT}$.

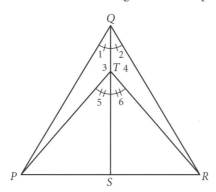

▶ **Solution**    First, you'll show that $\triangle PQT \cong \triangle RQT$ and then use CPCTC to show that $\overline{PT} \cong \overline{RT}$. You are given that $\angle 1 \cong \angle 2$. You also know that $\overline{QT} \cong \overline{QT}$ because they are the same segment. Now, because $\angle 3$ and $\angle 5$ are a linear pair, $m\angle 3 + m\angle 5 = 180°$, or equivalently, $m\angle 3 = 180° - m\angle 5$. Because $\angle 5 \cong \angle 6$, you can substitute $m\angle 6$ for $m\angle 5$ to get $m\angle 3 = 180° - m\angle 6$.

However, $\angle 4$ and $\angle 6$ form a linear pair, so $m\angle 4$ is also equal to $180° - m\angle 6$. Therefore, $m\angle 3 = m\angle 4$. That is, $\angle 3 \cong \angle 4$. So, by ASA, $\triangle PQT \cong \triangle RQT$. Because the triangles are congruent, $\overline{PT} \cong \overline{RT}$ by CPCTC.

When you are trying to prove that triangles are congruent, it can be hard to keep track of the information. Be sure to mark all the information on the figure. If the triangles are hard to see, you can draw them with different colors or redraw them separately. These techniques are demonstrated in Example B in your book. Read that example and make sure you understand it. Then read the example on the next page.

(continued)

**EXAMPLE B**     Is $\overline{AC} \cong \overline{DB}$? Write a paragraph proof explaining why.

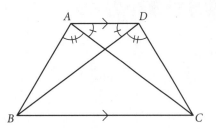

▶ **Solution**     You can draw triangles *ABC* and *DCB* separately to see them more clearly. As
you discover more information, mark it on the original diagram and the
separated triangles.

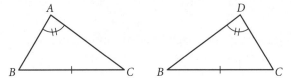

**Paragraph Proof:** Show that $\overline{AC} \cong \overline{DB}$.

$\angle BAC \cong \angle CDB$. Also, $\overline{BC} \cong \overline{CB}$ because they are the same segment.
Because $\overline{AD} \parallel \overline{BC}$, the alternate interior angles are congruent. Therefore,
$\angle ACB \cong \angle DAC$ and $\angle ADB \cong \angle DBC$. Because it is given that $\angle DAC \cong \angle ADB$,
it must also be true that $\angle ACB \cong \angle DBC$. (Mark this information on the
diagrams.) $\triangle ABC \cong \triangle DCB$ by SAA. By CPCTC, $\overline{AC} \cong \overline{DB}$.

# Flowchart Thinking

In this lesson you will

- Write **flowchart proofs**

So far, you have been writing explanations as deductive arguments or paragraph proofs. Example A in your book shows a paragraph proof. Read this example and make sure you understand the proof.

When a logical argument is complex or includes many steps, a paragraph proof may not be the clearest way to present the steps. In such cases, it is often helpful to organize the steps in the form of a *flowchart*. A **flowchart** is a visual way to organize all the steps in a complicated procedure in their proper order. The steps in the procedure are written in boxes. Arrows connect the boxes to show how facts lead to conclusions.

Creating a **flowchart proof** makes your logic visible so that others can follow your reasoning. Example B in your book presents the argument from Example A in flowchart form. Read the proof carefully. Notice that each statement is written in a box and that the logical reason for each step is written beneath its box.

More flowchart proofs are given in the examples below. In each example, try to write a proof yourself before looking at the solution. Remember, there are often several ways to prove a statement. Your proof may not be the same as the one given.

**EXAMPLE A** | **Given:** $\overline{MP}$ is a median
$\angle N \cong \angle Q$

**Show:** $\angle NMP \cong \angle QMP$

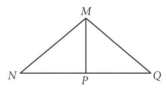

▷ **Solution** | **Flowchart Proof**

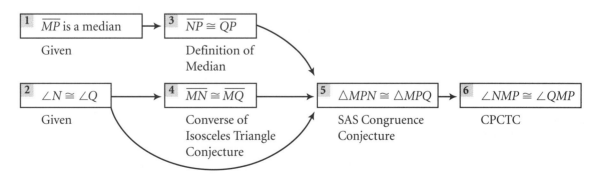

(continued)

**EXAMPLE B**

**Given:** $\overline{AE} \parallel \overline{CD}$
$B$ is the midpoint of $\overline{CE}$

**Show:** $\overline{AB} \cong \overline{DB}$

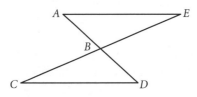

▶ **Solution** │ **Flowchart Proof**

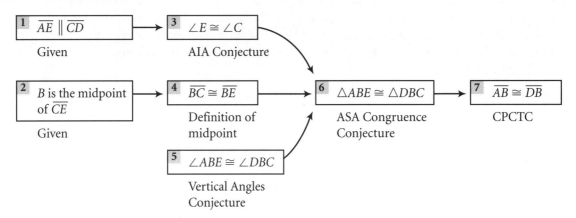

1. $\overline{AE} \parallel \overline{CD}$

   Given

2. $B$ is the midpoint of $\overline{CE}$

   Given

3. $\angle E \cong \angle C$

   AIA Conjecture

4. $\overline{BC} \cong \overline{BE}$

   Definition of midpoint

5. $\angle ABE \cong \angle DBC$

   Vertical Angles Conjecture

6. $\triangle ABE \cong \triangle DBC$

   ASA Congruence Conjecture

7. $\overline{AB} \cong \overline{DB}$

   CPCTC

# Proving Special Triangle Conjectures

In this lesson you will

- Make a conjecture about the bisector of the vertex angle in an isosceles triangle
- Make and prove a conjecture about equilateral triangles
- Learn about **biconditional** conjectures

In △ARC, $\overline{CD}$ is the altitude to the base $\overline{AR}$, $\overline{CE}$ is the angle bisector of ∠ACR, and $\overline{CF}$ is the median to side $\overline{AR}$. This example illustrates that the angle bisector, the altitude, and the median can all be different segments. Is this always true? Can they all be the same segment? You will explore these questions in the investigation.

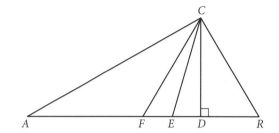

## Investigation: The Symmetry Line in an Isosceles Triangle

Construct a large isosceles triangle on a sheet of unlined paper. Label it *ARK*, with *K* as the vertex angle.

Construct angle bisector $\overline{KD}$ with point *D* on $\overline{AR}$. Compare △ADK with △RDK. Do they look congruent?

Use your compass to compare $\overline{AD}$ and $\overline{RD}$. Are they congruent? If so, then *D* is the midpoint of $\overline{AR}$, and therefore $\overline{KD}$ is the median to $\overline{AR}$. Notice that ∠ADK and ∠RDK are a linear pair and are therefore supplementary. Now compare ∠ADK and ∠RDK. Are the angles congruent? If so, what must the measure of each angle be? What does this tell you about $\overline{KD}$ and $\overline{AR}$?

Your findings should lead to the following conjecture.

> **Vertex Angle Bisector Conjecture** In an isosceles triangle, the bisector of the vertex angle is also the altitude and the median to the base.    **C-27**

In Chapter 3, you discovered that if a triangle is equilateral, then each angle measures 60°. Therefore, if a triangle is equilateral, then it is equiangular. This is called the Equilateral Triangle Conjecture. A proof of this statement is given on page 245 of your book. Read this proof carefully and make sure you understand each step. The *converse* of this statement is also true. That is, if a triangle is equiangular, then it is equilateral. The following conjecture combines these ideas.

> **Equilateral/Equiangular Triangle Conjecture** Every equilateral triangle is equiangular, and, conversely, every equiangular triangle is equilateral.    **C-28**

(continued)

A **biconditional** conjecture is a conjecture in which one condition cannot be true unless the other is also true. In other words, both the statement and its converse are true. The Equilateral/Equiangular Triangle Conjecture is biconditional, so it can be written: A triangle is equilateral *if and only if* it is equiangular.

Here is an example using the new conjectures.

**EXAMPLE** | $\triangle DEF$ is isosceles with $\overline{DF} \cong \overline{EF}$.

**a.** $m\angle D = 67°$
$DE = 15$ cm
$m\angle DFP =$ _____
$DP =$ _____

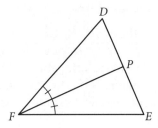

**b.** $m\angle DFE = 54°$
$DP = 7$ cm
$m\angle DFP =$ _____
$DE =$ _____

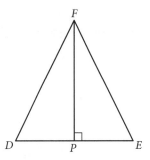

▶ **Solution** | **a.** If $m\angle D = 67°$, then $m\angle E = 67°$ because $\angle D$ and $\angle E$ are base angles of an isosceles triangle. Therefore, $m\angle DFE = 180° - (67° + 67°) = 46°$. Because $\overline{FP}$ bisects $\angle DFE$, $m\angle DFP = \frac{1}{2}(46°) = 23°$.

Because $\overline{FP}$ bisects vertex angle $DFE$, it must also be the median to $\overline{DE}$. Therefore, $DP = \frac{1}{2}DE = \frac{1}{2}(15 \text{ cm}) = 7.5$ cm.

**b.** Because $\overline{FP}$ is the altitude to $\overline{DE}$, it must also be the bisector of vertex angle $DFE$. Therefore, $m\angle DFP = \frac{1}{2}(m\angle DFE) = \frac{1}{2}(54°) = 27°$.

Because $\overline{FP}$ bisects vertex angle $DFE$, it must also be the median to $\overline{DE}$. Therefore, $DE = 2DP = 2(7 \text{ cm}) = 14$ cm.

# Polygon Sum Conjecture

In this lesson you will

- Discover a formula for finding the **sum of the angle measures** for any **polygon**
- Use **deductive reasoning** to explain why the polygon sum formula works

Triangles come in many different shapes and sizes. However, as you discovered in Chapter 4, the sum of the angle measures of any triangle is 180°. In this lesson you will investigate the sum of the angle measures of other polygons. After you find a pattern, you'll write a formula that relates the number of sides of a polygon to the sum of the measures of its angles.

## Investigation: Is There a Polygon Sum Formula?

Draw three different quadrilaterals. For each quadrilateral, carefully measure the four angles and then find the sum of the angle measures. If you measure carefully, you should find that all of your quadrilaterals have the same angle sum. What is the sum? Record it in a table like the one below.

| Number of sides | 3 | 4 | 5 | 6 | 7 | 8 | . . . | $n$ |
|---|---|---|---|---|---|---|---|---|
| Sum of angle measures | 180° | | | | 900° | 1080° | | |

Next draw three different pentagons. Carefully measure the angles in each pentagon and find the angle sum. Again, you should find that the angle sum is the same for each pentagon. Record the sum in the table.

Use your findings to complete the conjectures below.

> **Quadrilateral Sum Conjecture** The sum of the measures of the four angles **C-29** of any quadrilateral is _____.

> **Pentagon Sum Conjecture** The sum of the measures of the five angles of **C-30** any pentagon is _____.

Now draw at least two different hexagons and find their angle sum. Record the sum in the table.

The angle sums for heptagons and octagons have been entered in the table for you, but you can check the sums by drawing and measuring your own polygons.

Look for a pattern in the completed table. Find a general formula for the sum of the angle measures of a polygon in terms of the number of sides, $n$. (*Hint:* Use what you learned in Chapter 2 about finding the formula for a pattern with a constant difference.) Then complete this conjecture.

> **Polygon Sum Conjecture** The sum of the measures of the $n$ interior angles **C-31** of an $n$-gon is _____.

(continued)

You can use deductive reasoning to see why your formula works. In each polygon below, all the diagonals from one vertex have been drawn, creating triangles. Notice that in each polygon, the number of triangles is 2 less than the number of sides.

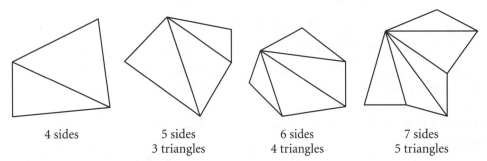

| 4 sides | 5 sides | 6 sides | 7 sides |
| | 3 triangles | 4 triangles | 5 triangles |

The quadrilateral has been divided into two triangles, each with an angle sum of 180°. So, the angle sum for the quadrilateral is 180° · 2, or 360°. The pentagon has been divided into three triangles, so its angle sum is 180° · 3, or 540°. The angle sums for the hexagon and the heptagon are 180° · 4 and 180° · 5, respectively. In general, if a polygon has $n$ sides, its angle sum is $180°(n - 2)$ or, equivalently, $180°n - 360°$. This should agree with the formula you found earlier.

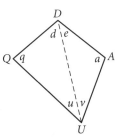

You can use the diagram at right to write a paragraph proof of the Quadrilateral Sum Conjecture. See if you can fill in the steps in the proof below.

**Paragraph Proof:** Show that $m\angle Q + m\angle U + m\angle A + m\angle D = 360°$.

$q + d + u = 180°$ and $e + a + v = 180°$ by the _____ Conjecture. By the Addition Property of Equality, $q + d + u + e + a + v =$ _____. Therefore, the sum of the angle measures of a quadrilateral is 360°.

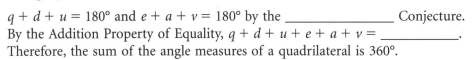

Here is an example using your new conjectures.

**EXAMPLE** | Find the lettered angle measures.

a.
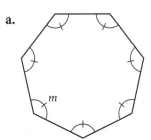

b.
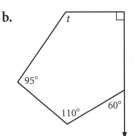

▶ **Solution** | a. The polygon has seven sides, so the angle sum is 180° · 5, or 900°. Because all the angles have the same measure, the measure of angle $m$ is 900° ÷ 7, or about 128.6°.

b. The polygon has five sides, so the angle sum is 180° · 3, or 540°. Therefore, $90° + 120° + 110° + 95° + t = 540°$. Solving for $t$ gives $t = 125°$.

# 5.2 Exterior Angles of a Polygon

In this lesson you will

- Find the sum of the measures of one set of **exterior angles** of a polygon
- Derive two formulas for the measure of each angle of an equiangular polygon

In Lesson 5.1, you discovered a formula for the sum of the measures of the *interior* angles of any polygon. In this lesson, you will find a formula for the sum of the measures of a set of *exterior* angles.

To create a set of exterior angles of a polygon, extend each side of the polygon to form one exterior angle at each vertex.

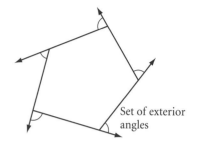

Set of exterior angles

### Investigation: Is There an Exterior Angle Sum?

Draw a triangle and extend its sides to form a set of exterior angles.

Measure two of the *interior* angles of your triangle. Then use the Triangle Sum Conjecture to find the measure of the remaining angle. Label each angle in your triangle with its measure.

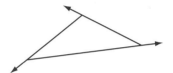

Use the Linear Pair Conjecture to calculate the measure of each exterior angle. Then find the sum of the exterior angle measures. Record your result in a table like the one below. Do you think you would get the same result for a different triangle? Draw another triangle and see.

| Number of sides | 3 | 4 | 5 | 6 | 7 | 8 | ... | n |
|---|---|---|---|---|---|---|---|---|
| Sum of exterior angle measures | 360° | | | | | | ... | |

Next, draw a quadrilateral and create a set of exterior angles. Use a procedure similar to the one you used for triangles to find the sum of the set of exterior angles. Add your result to the table.

Next, find the sum of the exterior angles for a pentagon. Are you starting to see a pattern? Predict the sum of the exterior angle measures for a hexagon. Then draw a hexagon and check your prediction. Add your results to the table.

You should have discovered that, no matter how many sides a polygon has, the sum of its exterior angle measures is 360°. This can be stated as a conjecture.

---

**Exterior Angle Sum Conjecture** For any polygon, the sum of the measures of a set of exterior angles is 360°.  **C-32**

---

Look at the software construction on page 263 of your book. Notice that the exterior angles stay the same as the polygon shrinks to a point. How does this demonstrate the Exterior Angle Sum Conjecture?

(continued)

Now you will find two formulas for the measure of each *interior* angle in an equiangular polygon with *n* sides. Remember, an equiangular polygon is a polygon in which all angles have the same measure.

You can use the Polygon Sum Conjecture to derive the first formula. That conjecture states that the sum of the interior angle measures in a polygon with *n* sides is $180°(n - 2)$. If the polygon is equiangular, then each of the *n* angles has the same measure. Use these facts to write a formula for the measure of each angle.

To derive the second formula, you can use the Exterior Angle Sum Conjecture. According to that conjecture, the sum of the measures of the *n* exterior angles of a polygon is 360°. In an equiangular polygon, each of the exterior angles has the same measure. So, the measure of each exterior angle is $\frac{360°}{n}$. If each exterior angle measures $\frac{360°}{n}$, what must be the measure of each interior angle?

You can state your findings in a conjecture.

> **Equiangular Polygon Conjecture** You can find the measure of each | **C-33**
> interior angle in an equiangular *n*-gon by using either of these formulas:
> $180° - \frac{360°}{n}$ or $\frac{180°(n - 2)}{n}$.

**EXAMPLE** | Find the lettered angle measures.

a.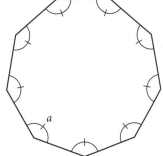

b.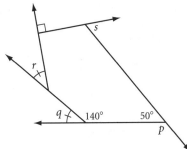

▶ **Solution** | a. This is an equiangular 9-gon. You can use the Equiangular Polygon Conjecture to find the measure of *a*.

$$a = 180° - \frac{360°}{9} = 180° - 40° = 140°$$

b. By the Linear Pair Conjecture, $p = 130°$ and $q = 40°$ so $r = 40°$ as well. To find *s*, use the Exterior Angle Sum Conjecture.

$$130° + 40° + 40° + 90° + s = 360°$$

Solving this equation gives $s = 60°$.

# 5.3 Kite and Trapezoid Properties

In this lesson you will

- Investigate the properties of **kites**
- Investigate properties of **trapezoids** and **isosceles trapezoids**

In this lesson you will look at two special types of quadrilaterals, kites and trapezoids. Recall that a **kite** is a quadrilateral with two distinct pairs of congruent consecutive sides.

You can make a kite by constructing two different isosceles triangles on opposite sides of a common base and then removing the base. In an isosceles triangle, the angle between the two congruent sides is called the vertex angle. For this reason, we'll call angles between the pairs of congruent sides of a kite **vertex angles.** We'll refer to the other two angles as **nonvertex angles.**

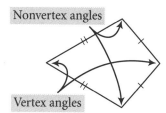
Nonvertex angles

Vertex angles

A kite has one line of reflectional symmetry, just like an isosceles triangle. You can use this property to discover other properties of kites.

## Investigation 1: What Are Some Properties of Kites?

Follow Step 1 in your book to construct a kite on patty paper.

Compare each angle to the opposite angle by folding. Which angles are congruent, vertex angles or nonvertex angles? Use your findings to complete this conjecture.

> **Kite Angles Conjecture** The _____ angles of a kite are congruent. **C-34**

Draw the diagonals of the kite. Fold the kite along one of the diagonals. The two parts of the other diagonal should coincide. What can you conclude about the angle between the diagonals? You are now ready to complete this conjecture.

> **Kite Diagonals Conjecture** The diagonals of a kite are _____. **C-35**

Now fold along each diagonal and compare the lengths of the segments on the diagonals. Does either diagonal bisect the other? Complete this conjecture.

> **Kite Diagonal Bisector Conjecture** The diagonal connecting the vertex angles of a kite is the _____ of the other diagonal. **C-36**

Fold along the diagonal connecting the vertex angles. Does the diagonal bisect the vertex angles? Now fold along the other diagonal. Does it bisect the nonvertex angles? Complete this conjecture.

> **Kite Angle Bisector Conjecture** The _____ angles of a kite are bisected by a diagonal. **C-37**

(continued)

Now you will explore some properties of trapezoids. Recall that a **trapezoid** is a quadrilateral with exactly one pair of parallel sides. The parallel sides are called **bases**. A pair of angles that share a base as a common side are called **base angles**.

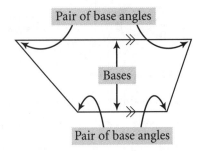

### Investigation 2: What Are Some Properties of Trapezoids?

Follow Steps 1 and 2 in your book. Use your findings to complete this conjecture.

**Trapezoid Consecutive Angles Conjecture** The consecutive angles    **C-38**
between the bases of a trapezoid are _____.

An **isosceles trapezoid** is a trapezoid whose nonparallel sides are the same length. An isosceles trapezoid has a line of symmetry that passes through the midpoints of the two bases.

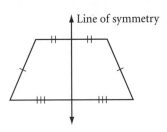

Use both edges of your straightedge to draw parallel segments. To construct the congruent sides, make identical arcs centered at the endpoints of one of the segments so that each arc intersects the other segment. Then connect points as shown below to form the trapezoid.

Measure each pair of base angles. How do the angles in each pair compare? Complete this conjecture.

**Isosceles Trapezoid Conjecture** The base angles of an isosceles trapezoid    **C-39**
are _____.

Now draw the two diagonals. Compare their lengths and complete this conjecture.

**Isosceles Trapezoid Diagonals Conjecture** The diagonals of an isosceles    **C-40**
trapezoid are _____.

Follow the Developing Proof instructions on page 271 of your book and complete a flowchart proof of the Isosceles Trapezoid Diagonals Conjecture, using the Isosceles Trapezoid Conjecture and congruent triangles. Separating the triangles as shown at right might help you. Remember to mark congruent parts on your diagram.

 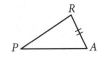

# 5.4 Properties of Midsegments

## CONDENSED LESSON

In this lesson you will

- Discover properties of the **midsegment** of a **triangle**
- Discover properties of the **midsegment** of a **trapezoid**

In Chapter 3, you learned that a *midsegment* of a triangle is a segment connecting the midpoints of two sides. In this lesson you will investigate properties of midsegments.

### Investigation 1: Triangle Midsegment Properties

Follow Steps 1–3 in your book. Your conclusions should lead to the following conjecture.

> **Three Midsegments Conjecture** The three midsegments of a triangle divide it into four congruent triangles.
>
> **C-41**

Mark all the congruent angles in your triangle as shown in this example.

Focus on one of the midsegments and the third side of the triangle (the side the midsegment doesn't intersect). Look at the pairs of alternate interior angles and corresponding angles associated with these segments. What conclusion can you make? Look at the angles associated with each of the other midsegments and the corresponding third side.

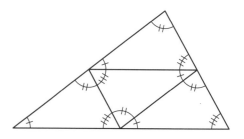

Now compare the length of each midsegment to the length of the corresponding third side. How are the lengths related?

State your findings in the form of a conjecture.

> **Triangle Midsegment Conjecture** A midsegment of a triangle is _____ to the third side and _____ the length of the third side.
>
> **C-42**

The midsegment of a trapezoid is the segment connecting the midpoints of the two nonparallel sides.

### Investigation 2: Trapezoid Midsegment Properties

Follow Steps 1–3 in your book. You should find that the trapezoid's base angles are congruent to the corresponding angles at the midsegment. What can you conclude about the relationship of the midsegment to the bases?

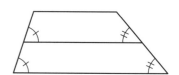

Now follow Steps 5–7. You should find that the midsegment fits twice onto the segment representing the sum of the two bases. That is, the length of the

(continued)

midsegment is half the sum of the lengths of the two bases. Another way to say this is: The length of the midsegment is the average of the lengths of the bases.

Use what you have learned about the midsegment of a trapezoid to complete this conjecture.

---

**Trapezoid Midsegment Conjecture** The midsegment of a trapezoid    **C-43**
is _____ to the bases and equal in length to _____.

---

Read the text below the investigation on page 277 of your book and study the software construction. Make sure you understand the relationship between the Trapezoid and Triangle Midsegment Conjectures.

Work through the following example yourself before checking the solution.

**EXAMPLE** | Find the lettered measures.

a.
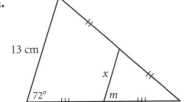

b.
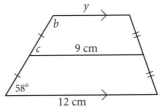

▶ **Solution** | a. By the Triangle Midsegment Conjecture, $x = \frac{1}{2}(13 \text{ cm}) = 6.5 \text{ cm}$.

The Triangle Midsegment Conjecture also tells you that the midsegment is parallel to the third side. Therefore, the corresponding angles are congruent, so $m = 72°$.

b. By the Trapezoid Midsegment Conjecture, $\frac{1}{2}(12 + y) = 9$. Solving for $y$ gives $y = 6$.

The Trapezoid Midsegment Conjecture also tells you that the midsegment is parallel to the bases. Therefore, the corresponding angles are congruent, so $c = 58°$.

By the Trapezoid Consecutive Angles Conjecture, $b + 58° = 180°$, so $b = 122°$.

# 5.5 Properties of Parallelograms

In this lesson you will

- Discover how the **angles** of a parallelogram are related
- Discover how the **sides** of a parallelogram are related
- Discover how the **diagonals** of a parallelogram are related

You have explored properties of kites and trapezoids and of the midsegments of triangles and trapezoids. In this lesson you will explore properties of parallelograms.

### Investigation: Four Parallelogram Properties

Follow the directions in Step 1 in your book to construct and label a parallelogram.

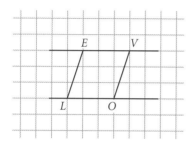

Use patty paper or a protractor to compare the measures of the opposite angles. Then use your findings to complete this conjecture.

> **Parallelogram Opposite Angles Conjecture** The opposite angles of a **C-44**
> parallelogram are _____.

Consecutive angles are angles that share a common side. In parallelogram *LOVE*, ∠*LOV* and ∠*EVO* are one pair of consecutive angles. There are three other pairs. Find the sum of the measures of each pair of consecutive angles. You should find that the sum is the same for all four pairs. What is the sum? Complete this conjecture.

> **Parallelogram Consecutive Angles Conjecture** The consecutive angles of **C-45**
> a parallelogram are _____.

Suppose you are given the measure of one angle of a parallelogram. Describe how you can use the conjectures above to find the measures of the other three angles. If you don't know, look at this particular figure. What are the values of *a*, *b*, and *c*? (Remember all your parallel lines conjectures.)

(continued)

Use a compass or patty paper to compare the lengths of the opposite sides of your parallelogram. How are the lengths related? Complete this conjecture.

**Parallelogram Opposite Sides Conjecture** The opposite sides of a parallelogram are _____.

**C-46**

Now draw the diagonals of your parallelogram. Label the point where the diagonals intersect *M*. How do *LM* and *VM* compare? How do *EM* and *OM* compare? What does this tell you about the relationship between the diagonals? Complete this conjecture.

**Parallelogram Diagonals Conjecture** The diagonals of a parallelogram _____ each other.

**C-47**

In your book, read the text about **vectors** that follows the investigation.

Here is an example using your new conjectures.

**EXAMPLE** | In parts a and b, the figures are parallelograms. Find the lettered measures and state which conjectures you used.

**a.**
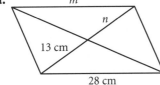

**b.**

▶ **Solution** | **a.** By the Parallelogram Opposite Sides Conjecture, *m* = 28 cm.
By the Parallelogram Diagonals Conjecture, *n* = 13 cm.

**b.** By the Parallelogram Opposite Angles Conjecture, *t* = 112°.
By the Parallelogram Consecutive Angles Conjecture, *s* = 180° − 112° = 68°.

# Properties of Special Parallelograms

In this lesson you will

- Discover properties of **rhombuses** and their diagonals
- Discover properties of **rectangles** and their diagonals
- Discover properties of **squares** and their diagonals

In Lesson 5.5, you investigated parallelograms. In this lesson you focus on three special parallelograms—rhombuses, rectangles, and squares.

## Investigation 1: What Can You Draw With the Double-Edged Straightedge?

Follow Steps 1–3 in your book. You should find that all the sides of the parallelogram you create are the same length. Use your findings to complete this conjecture.

> **Double-Edged Straightedge Conjecture** If two parallel lines are intersected by a second pair of parallel lines that are the same distance apart as the first pair, then the parallelogram formed is a _____. **C-48**

Now that you know a quick way to construct a rhombus, you will explore some special properties of rhombuses.

## Investigation 2: Do Rhombus Diagonals Have Special Properties?

In this investigation you will look at the diagonals of a rhombus. Follow Steps 1 and 2 in your book. Then complete this conjecture.

> **Rhombus Diagonals Conjecture** The diagonals of a rhombus are _____ and they _____ each other. **C-49**

Follow Step 3 to compare the two angles formed at each vertex by a diagonal and the sides. Then complete this conjecture.

> **Rhombus Angles Conjecture** The diagonals of a rhombus _____ the angles of the rhombus. **C-50**

You have just explored rhombuses, parallelograms with four congruent sides. Now you will look at rectangles, parallelograms with four congruent angles.

By the Quadrilateral Sum Conjecture, you know that the sum of the angle measures of a rectangle is 360°. Because all the angles have the same measures, each angle must have measure 90°. In other words, a rectangle has four right angles.

(continued)

### Investigation 3: Do Rectangle Diagonals Have Special Properties?

Follow Steps 1 and 2 in your book. What do you notice about the lengths of the two diagonals? Because a rectangle is a parallelogram, you also know that the diagonals bisect each other. You can use your compass to confirm this for your rectangle. Combine these two observations to complete the conjecture.

> **Rectangle Diagonals Conjecture** The diagonals of a rectangle
> are _____ and _____ each other.
>
> `C-51`

A square is a parallelogram that is both equiangular and equilateral. Here are two definitions of a square.

A **square** is an equiangular rhombus.

A **square** is an equilateral rectangle.

Because a square is a parallelogram, a rhombus, and a rectangle, all the properties of these quadrilaterals are also true for squares. Look back at what you know about the diagonals of each of these quadrilaterals, and use your findings to complete this conjecture.

> **Square Diagonals Conjecture** The diagonals of a square are
> _____, _____, and _____.
>
> `C-52`

**EXAMPLE** | Find the lettered measures.

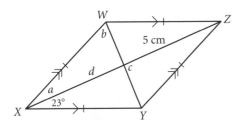

▶ **Solution** | The figure is a rhombus, so by the Rhombus Angles Conjecture, the diagonals bisect the angles. Therefore, $a = 23°$.

By the Parallelogram Consecutive Angles Conjecture, $\angle WXY$ and $\angle XWZ$ are supplementary, so $m\angle XWZ + 46° = 180°$. Therefore, $m\angle XWZ = 134°$. So, using the Rhombus Angles Conjecture, $b = \frac{1}{2}(134°) = 67°$.

By the Rhombus Diagonals Conjecture, the diagonals are perpendicular and bisect each other, so $c = 90°$ and $d = 5$ cm.

# 5.7 Proving Quadrilateral Properties

In this lesson you will

- Learn about the "thinking backward" strategy for writing proofs
- Prove many of the quadrilateral conjectures from this chapter

In this chapter you have made many conjectures about the properties of quadrilaterals. In this lesson you will write proofs for several of these conjectures.

Look at the illustration of the firefighters in your book. The firefighter holding the hose has asked the other firefighter to turn on one of the hydrants. Which one should he turn on? One way to solve this problem is to start with the end of the hose in the first firefighter's hand and trace it backward to a hydrant. You can use a similar strategy to help you write proofs.

To plan a proof, it often helps to start with the conclusion (that is, the statement you want to prove) and work your way back to the beginning, one step at a time. Making a flowchart can help you visualize the flow of reasoning. The example in your book illustrates how this strategy works. Read this example carefully. Then read the example below, which shows how to prove the statement in Exercise 3.

**EXAMPLE**  Prove the conjecture: If the opposite sides of a quadrilateral are congruent, then the quadrilateral is a parallelogram.

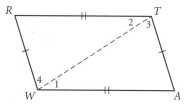

**Given:** Quadrilateral $WATR$ with $\overline{WA} \cong \overline{RT}$ and $\overline{WR} \cong \overline{AT}$, and diagonal $\overline{WT}$

**Show:** $WATR$ is a parallelogram

▶ **Solution**  Construct your proof by working backward. Your thinking might go something like this:

"I can show that $WATR$ is a parallelogram if I can show that the opposite sides are parallel. That is, I need to show that $\overline{RT} \parallel \overline{WA}$ and $\overline{WR} \parallel \overline{AT}$."

$$\boxed{\overline{RT} \parallel \overline{WA}} \longrightarrow \boxed{\begin{array}{c} WATR \text{ is a} \\ \text{parallelogram} \end{array}}$$

$$\boxed{\overline{WR} \parallel \overline{AT}} \longrightarrow$$

"I can show that $\overline{RT} \parallel \overline{WA}$ if I can show that the alternate interior angles $\angle 1$ and $\angle 2$ are congruent. I can show that $\overline{WR} \parallel \overline{AT}$ if I can show that the alternate interior angles $\angle 4$ and $\angle 3$ are congruent."

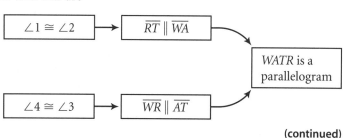

(continued)

"I can show that $\angle 1 \cong \angle 2$ and $\angle 4 \cong \angle 3$ if they are corresponding parts of congruent triangles."

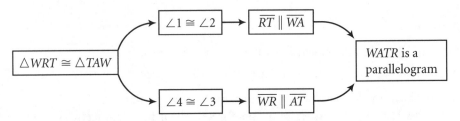

"Can I show that $\triangle WRT \cong \triangle TAW$? Yes, I can, by SSS, because it is given that $\overline{WA} \cong \overline{RT}$ and $\overline{WR} \cong \overline{AT}$, and $\overline{WT} \cong \overline{WT}$ because it is the same segment in both triangles."

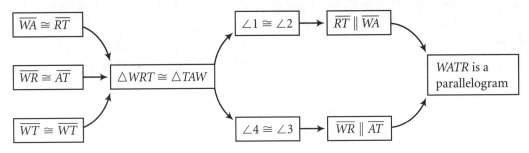

By adding the reason for each statement below each box, you can make the flowchart into a complete flowchart proof.

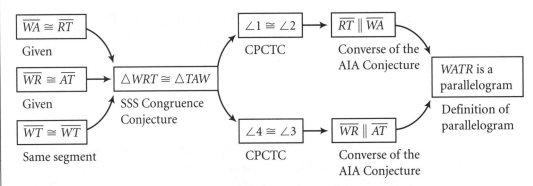

If you prefer, you can write the proof in paragraph form:

"It is given that $\overline{WA} \cong \overline{RT}$ and $\overline{WR} \cong \overline{AT}$. $\overline{WT} \cong \overline{WT}$ because it is the same segment. So, $\triangle WRT \cong \triangle TAW$ by the SSS Congruence Conjecture. By CPCTC, $\angle 1 \cong \angle 2$ and $\angle 4 \cong \angle 3$. By the converse of the Alternate Interior Angles Conjecture, $\overline{RT} \parallel \overline{WA}$ and $\overline{WR} \parallel \overline{AT}$. Therefore, WATR is a parallelogram because, by definition, a parallelogram is a quadrilateral in which the opposite sides are parallel. Q.E.D."

For more practice with working backward, work through the Finding the Square Route Investigation on page 300 of your book.

# Tangent Properties

In this lesson you will

- Review terms associated with **circles**
- Discover how a tangent to a circle and the radius to the **point of tangency** are related
- Make a conjecture about **tangent segments** to a circle from a point outside the circle

You have already learned some terms related to circles. Review them by matching the terms and figures on page 310 of your book.

The **tangent** to a circle is a line in the plane of the circle that intersects the circle in exactly one point. The point where the tangent touches the circle is the **point of tangency.**

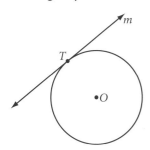

Line *m* is a **tangent** to circle *O*.
Point *T* is the **point of tangency.**

## Investigation 1: Going Off on a Tangent

Construct a large circle. Label the center *O*.

Use a straightedge to draw a line that appears to touch the circle at one point. Label the point *T* and draw radius $\overline{OT}$.

Measure the angles formed by the radius and the tangent line. How do the angles compare?

Will you get the same result with a different tangent? Draw another tangent and see. Use your findings to complete this conjecture.

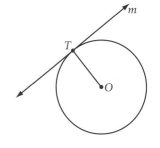

**Tangent Conjecture** A tangent to a circle is _____ to the radius drawn to the point of tangency.  `C-53`

## Investigation 2: Tangent Segments

Follow Steps 1–3 in your book. How do the lengths of the tangent segments compare?

Will you get the same results if you start with a different point outside the circle? Choose another point and see. Use your findings to complete this conjecture.

**Tangent Segments Conjecture** Tangent segments to a circle from a point outside the circle are _____.  `C-54`

(continued)

Read the information about minor and major arcs on page 313 of your book, and study the example. Then read about **internally tangent circles** and **externally tangent circles**.

Now read the example below.

**EXAMPLE**

a. $\overline{MN}$ and $\overline{MP}$ are tangents to circle $O$.

$x =$ _____

$y =$ _____

$m\widehat{NP} =$ _____

$m\widehat{PQN} =$ _____

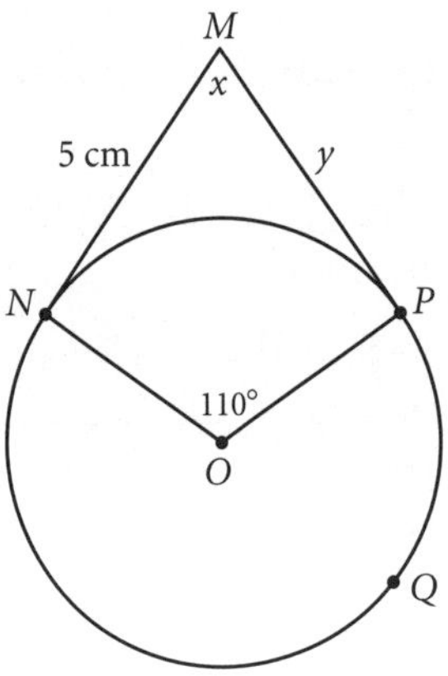

5 cm

110°

b. $\overleftrightarrow{AD}$ is tangent to both circle $B$ and circle $C$.

$w =$ _____

$m\widehat{AXT} =$ _____

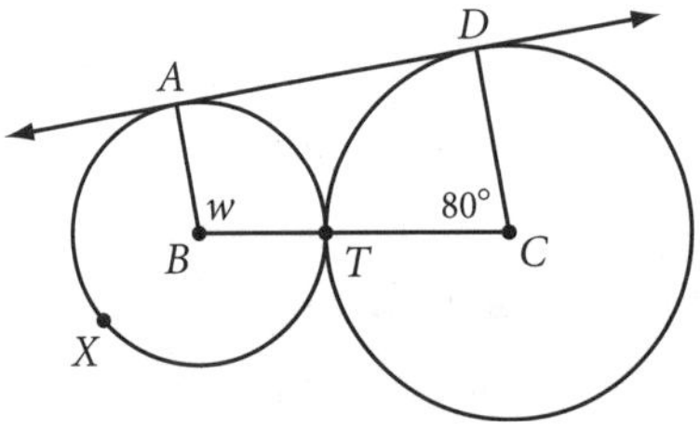

80°

c. Refer to the figure for part a. What type of quadrilateral is $MNOP$?

▶ **Solution**

a. By the Tangent Conjecture, $m\angle MNO = 90°$ and $m\angle MPO = 90°$. By the Quadrilateral Sum Conjecture, $90° + 90° + 110° + x = 360°$, so $x = 70°$. By the Tangent Segments Conjecture, $\overline{MN} \cong \overline{MP}$, so $y = 5$ cm.

Because the measure of a minor arc equals the measure of its central angle, $m\widehat{NP} = 110°$. Subtract this measure from 360° to find the measure of the major arc, giving $m\widehat{PQN} = 250°$.

b. By the Tangent Conjecture, $m\angle BAD = 90°$ and $m\angle CDA = 90°$. By the Quadrilateral Sum Conjecture, $90° + 90° + 80° + w = 360°$, so $w = 100°$.

The measure of minor arc $AT$ equals the measure of the central angle $\angle ABT$, so $m\widehat{AT} = 100°$. Subtract this measure from 360° to find the measure of its major arc: $m\widehat{AXT} = 360° - 100° = 260°$.

c. $MNOP$ is a kite because $\overline{MN} \cong \overline{MP}$ and $\overline{ON} \cong \overline{OP}$.

In this lesson you will

- Define **central angle** and **inscribed angle**
- Investigate properties of **chords** of a circle

## Investigation 1: Defining Angles in a Circle

In your book, look at the examples and non-examples of central angles. What do the central angles have in common? What characteristics do the central angles have that the other angles do not have? Use your observations to complete this definition of a central angle.

A **central angle** is an angle whose vertex is _____.

Now look at the examples and non-examples of inscribed angles. Notice that each inscribed angle has its vertex on the circle. However, so does ∠*VWX*, which is *not* an inscribed angle. What makes the inscribed angles different from ∠*VWX*? Use your findings to complete this definition.

An **inscribed angle** is an angle whose vertex is _____ and whose sides _____ .

## Investigation 2: Chords and Their Central Angles

Construct a large circle and label its center *O*. Use your compass to construct two congruent chords. Label the chords $\overline{AB}$ and $\overline{CD}$. Construct radii $\overline{OA}$, $\overline{OB}$, $\overline{OC}$, and $\overline{OD}$.

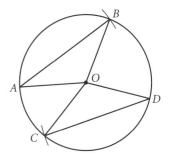

Use a protractor to measure ∠*BOA* and ∠*COD*. How do the measures compare?

See if you get the same results if you start with a different circle. Then complete this conjecture.

---
**Chord Central Angles Conjecture** If two chords in a circle are congruent, **C-55**
then they determine two central angles that are _____.
---

You learned in Lesson 6.1 that a minor arc has the same measure as its central angle. If chords $\overline{AB}$ and $\overline{CD}$ are congruent and central angles ∠*BOA* and ∠*COD* are congruent, what can you conclude about their intercepted arcs, $\overset{\frown}{AB}$ and $\overset{\frown}{CD}$?

You can fold your paper to confirm your answer. Now complete the conjecture.

---
**Chord Arcs Conjecture** If two chords in a circle are congruent, then their **C-56**
_____ are congruent.
---

(continued)

### Investigation 3: Chords and the Center of the Circle

Follow Step 1 in your book. The perpendicular to each chord divides the chord into two segments. How do the lengths of the segments compare? Use your findings to complete this conjecture.

> **Perpendicular to a Chord Conjecture** The perpendicular from the center **C-57** of a circle to a chord is the _____ of the chord.

Now use your compass to compare the distances (measured along the perpendicular) from the center to the chords. How do the distances compare?

Draw a circle of a different size and follow Step 1 in your book for the new circle. Compare the distances from the center of the circle to each chord. Are your findings the same as they were for the first circle? Complete the conjecture.

> **Chord Distance to Center Conjecture** Two congruent chords in a circle **C-58** are _____ from the center of the circle.

### Investigation 4: Perpendicular Bisector of a Chord

Construct a large circle and mark the center. Draw two nonparallel chords that are *not* diameters. Construct the perpendicular bisector of each chord and extend the bisectors until they intersect. Where is the point of intersection?

Construct another circle that is larger or smaller than the first circle you drew. Draw two chords and construct their perpendicular bisectors. Where do the perpendicular bisectors intersect? Complete this conjecture.

> **Perpendicular Bisector of a Chord Conjecture** The perpendicular bisector **C-59** of a chord passes through the _____ of the circle.

Now you can find the center of any circle and the vertex of the central angle of any arc. All you have to do is construct the perpendicular bisectors of nonparallel chords.

# 6.3 | Arcs and Angles

In this lesson you will

- Make conjectures about **inscribed angles** in a circle
- Investigate relationships among the angles in a **cyclic quadrilateral**
- Compare the arcs formed when two parallel lines intersect a circle

In this lesson you'll discover properties of arcs and the angles associated with them.

## Investigation 1: Inscribed Angle Properties

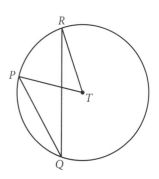

Refer to the diagram of circle $O$ in your book. Notice that $\angle COR$ is a *central angle*, while $\angle CAR$ is an *inscribed angle*. Both angles intercept $\overset{\frown}{CR}$.

Recall that the measure of a minor arc is equal to the measure of its central angle. Find $m\overset{\frown}{CR}$ by measuring $\angle COR$. Then find the measure of $\angle CAR$. How does the measure of the inscribed angle compare with the measure of its intercepted arc?

Construct your own circle $T$. Draw an inscribed angle $PQR$ and its corresponding central angle $PTR$. An example is shown at right.

What is the measure of $\overset{\frown}{PR}$? What is the measure of $\angle PQR$? How do the measures compare? Use your findings from this investigation to complete the conjecture.

> **Inscribed Angle Conjecture** The measure of an angle inscribed in a circle **C-60**
> is _____ the measure of its intercepted arc.

## Investigation 2: Inscribed Angles Intercepting the Same Arc

Follow Steps 1 and 2 in your book. Note that selecting $P$ and $Q$ on the major arc creates two angles, $\angle APB$ and $\angle AQB$, that intercept the same *minor arc*.

Draw another circle. Follow Step 4 in your book. Note that selecting $P$ and $Q$ on the minor arc creates two angles, $\angle APB$ and $\angle AQB$, that intercept the same *major arc*.

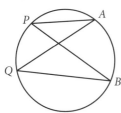
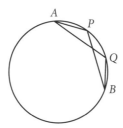

In each case, how do the measures of the two inscribed angles compare? Use your findings to complete the conjecture.

> **Inscribed Angles Intercepting Arcs Conjecture** Inscribed angles that **C-61**
> intercept the same arc are _____.

(continued)

### Investigation 3: Angles Inscribed in a Semicircle

Follow Steps 1 and 2 in your book to construct and measure three angles inscribed in the same semicircle. All the angles should have the same measure. What is the measure? Complete this conjecture.

**Angles Inscribed in a Semicircle Conjecture** Angles inscribed in a semicircle are _____.

**C-62**

### Investigation 4: Cyclic Quadrilaterals

A quadrilateral inscribed in a circle is called a **cyclic quadrilateral.**

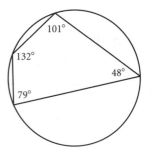

Construct a large circle. Choose four points on the circle and connect them to form a cyclic quadrilateral. Label each angle with its measure. In another circle, construct a second cyclic quadrilateral and label its angles with their measures. At right is one more example.

In each cyclic quadrilateral, find sums of pairs of consecutive angles and sums of pairs of opposite angles. What do you discover? Complete this conjecture.

**Cyclic Quadrilateral Conjecture** The _____ angles of a cyclic quadrilateral are _____.

**C-63**

### Investigation 5: Arcs by Parallel Lines

Read the definition of **secant** and follow Steps 1–3 in your book. Then complete the conjecture.

**Parallel Lines Intercepted Arcs Conjecture** Parallel lines intercept _____ arcs on a circle.

**C-64**

Read the example below.

**EXAMPLE**  Find each lettered measure.

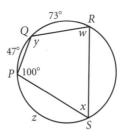

▶ **Solution**   By the Cyclic Quadrilateral Conjecture, $w + 100° = 180°$, so $w = 80°$. $\angle PSR$ intercepts $\overset{\frown}{PR}$. $m\overset{\frown}{PR} = 47° + 73° = 120°$, so by the Inscribed Angle Conjecture, $x = \frac{1}{2}(120°) = 60°$.

By the Cyclic Quadrilateral Conjecture, $x + y = 180°$. Substituting 60° for $x$ and solving the equation gives $y = 120°$. By the Inscribed Angle Conjecture, $w = \frac{1}{2}(47° + z)$. Substituting 80° for $w$ and solving the equation gives $z = 113°$.

# Proving Circle Conjectures

In this lesson you will

- Prove the **Inscribed Angle Conjecture**
- Prove other conjectures related to circles

In Lesson 6.3, you discovered the Inscribed Angle Conjecture.

> The measure of an inscribed angle in a circle equals half the measure of its intercepted arc.

In this lesson you will prove this conjecture. First, note that there are three ways an inscribed angle can relate to the circle's center.

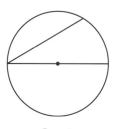

Case 1

The circle's center
is on the angle.

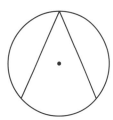

Case 2

The center is
outside the angle.

Case 3

The center is
inside the angle.

These are the only possibilities, so if you can prove the conjecture is true for each case, you will have proved the conjecture is always true.

## Case 1: The circle's center is on the inscribed angle.

Look at the drawing for Case 1 on page 330 of your book. The dashed radius $\overline{OA}$ has been added to form $\triangle AOB$. To prove the conjecture is true for this case, you need to show that $\angle ABC = \frac{1}{2}m\overset{\frown}{AC}$ $\left(\text{that is, } x = \frac{1}{2}m\overset{\frown}{AC}\right)$.

Notice the following things:

- $\angle AOC$ is the central angle for $\overset{\frown}{AC}$. (How are $z$ and $m\overset{\frown}{AC}$ related?)
- $\angle AOC$ is an exterior angle for $\triangle AOB$. (How are $x$, $y$, and $z$ related?)
- $\triangle AOB$ is isosceles. (How are $x$ and $y$ related?)

Combine these observations to write a flowchart proof for Case 1. Then, compare your proof with the one in your book.

## Case 2: The circle's center is outside the inscribed angle.

You can use Case 1 to help you prove Case 2. Look at the drawing for Case 2 on page 331 of your book. A dashed diameter, $\overline{DB}$, has been added. To prove the conjecture is true for this case, you must show that $m\angle ABC = \frac{1}{2}m\overset{\frown}{AC}$ $\left(\text{that is, } x = \frac{q}{2}\right)$.

Think about the following things:

- How are $x$, $y$, and $z$ related?
- How are $p$, $q$, and $m\overset{\frown}{DC}$ related?
- Using Case 1, how is $y$ related to $p$? How is $z$ related to $p + q$?

(continued)

Combine these observations to write a flowchart proof for Case 2. Then compare your proof with the one in your book.

**Case 3: The circle's center is inside the inscribed angle.**

Use the given information and the marked figure in Example A below to write a flowchart proof for this case. You may want to use your flowchart from Case 2 as a guide for this proof. Write your proof before you look at the solution to Example A. Then compare your proof with the one given.

**EXAMPLE A**

Prove Case 3 of the Inscribed Angle Conjecture: The measure of an inscribed angle in a circle equals half the measure of its intercepted arc when the center of the circle is inside the angle.

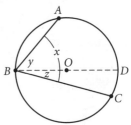

**Given:** Circle $O$ with inscribed angle $ABC$ whose sides lie on either side of diameter $BD$

**Show:** $m\angle ABC = \frac{1}{2}m\widehat{AC}$, or $x = \frac{1}{2}m\widehat{AC}$

▶ **Solution**

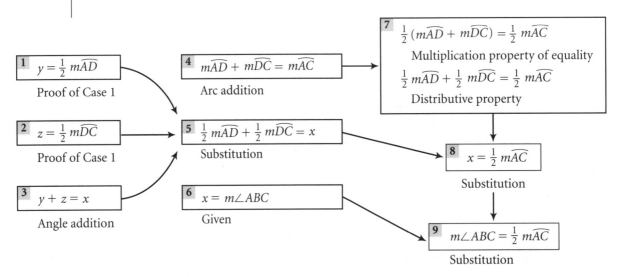

**EXAMPLE B**

Write a paragraph proof or a flowchart proof of the conjecture: If a kite is inscribed in a circle, then the nonvertex angles are right angles.

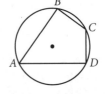

**Given:** Circle with inscribed kite $ABCD$ where $\overline{AB} \cong \overline{AD}$ and $\overline{BC} \cong \overline{CD}$

**Show:** $\angle B$ and $\angle D$ are right angles

▶ **Solution**

By the Kite Angles Conjecture, $\angle B \cong \angle D$. By the Cyclic Quadrilateral Conjecture, $\angle B$ and $\angle D$ are supplementary. Because $\angle B$ and $\angle D$ are both equal and supplementary, they must have measures of 90°. Therefore, $\angle B$ and $\angle D$ are right angles.

# 6.5 The Circumference/Diameter Ratio

In this lesson you will

- Discover the relationship between the **diameter** and the **circumference** of a circle

The distance around a polygon is called the perimeter. The distance around a circle is called the **circumference.**

Think of a can of three tennis balls. Which do you think is greater, the height of the can or the circumference of the can? The height is about three tennis-ball diameters, which is about the same as three can diameters. If you have a tennis-ball can, wrap a string around the can to measure the circumference, and then compare the measurement with the height. You should find that the circumference of the can is slightly greater than the height. That is, the circumference is a little more than three diameters. In the next investigation you will discover the relationship between the diameter and circumference of any circle.

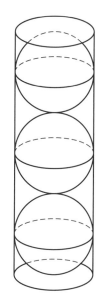

## Investigation: A Taste of Pi

For this investigation you will need several round objects, along with either a metric measuring tape or a string and a meterstick.

Wrap the measuring tape or string around each object to measure its circumference. Then measure the diameter of each object. Make all measurements to the nearest millimeter (tenth of a centimeter). The table below includes some sample measurements. Copy the table and add your findings to it.

| Object | Circumference (C) | Diameter (d) | Ratio $\frac{C}{d}$ |
|---|---|---|---|
| Quarter | 7.8 cm | 2.5 cm | |
| Compact disc | 37.7 cm | 12.0 cm | |
| Mug | 25.9 cm | 8.2 cm | |
| Small plate | 47.4 cm | 15.1 cm | |
| | | | |
| | | | |
| | | | |

Calculate the ratio $\frac{C}{d}$ for each object. You should find that, in each case, the ratio is a little more than 3. In fact, the ratio $\frac{C}{d}$ is exactly the same number for every circle. This constant ratio is denoted by the Greek letter $\pi$ (pi). So, $\frac{C}{d} = \pi$.

If you solve this equation for $C$, you get the formula for the circumference of a circle in terms of its diameter. Because the diameter of a circle is twice the radius, you can also write a formula for the circumference in terms of the radius.

---

**Circumference Conjecture** If $C$ is the circumference and $d$ is the diameter     **C-65**
of a circle, then there is a number $\pi$ such that $C =$ _____.
If $d = 2r$ where $r$ is the radius, then $C =$ _____.

---

(continued)

The number $\pi$ is an *irrational number,* so its decimal form never ends and its digits follow no pattern. Your calculator probably gives an approximation of $\pi$ to eight or nine decimal places. If you don't have access to a calculator, you can use the value 3.14 as an approximation for $\pi$. If you are asked to give an exact answer, state your answer in terms of $\pi$. The examples in your book show you how you can apply the Circumference Conjecture. Read the examples carefully. Here are two more examples.

**EXAMPLE A** | A circle has a radius of 6.5 meters. What is its circumference? Use a calculator and give your answer to the nearest 0.1 meter.

▸ **Solution** | $C = 2\pi r$      The formula for circumference.

$C = 2\pi(6.5)$      Substitute 6.5 for *r*.

$C = 13\pi \approx 40.8$ m      Evaluate and round to the nearest 0.1 m.

**EXAMPLE B** | To find your hat size, you measure the circumference of your head in inches, and then use the circumference formula to find the diameter to the nearest eighth of an inch. The circumference of Tameka's head is about $23\frac{1}{2}$ in. What is her hat size?

▸ **Solution** | $C = \pi d$    The formula for circumference.

$23\frac{1}{2} = \pi d$    Substitute $23\frac{1}{2}$ for *C*.

$7\frac{1}{2} \approx d$    Divide both sides by $\pi$ and round to the nearest eighth of an inch.

Tameka's hat size is $7\frac{1}{2}$.

*Discovering Geometry Condensed Lessons*
©2008 Key Curriculum Press

# Around the World

In this lesson you will

• Solve application problems involving radius, diameter, and circumference

Now that you have learned about $\pi$ and the formula for circumference, you can solve many real-world problems involving circles. The example in your book shows the solution to a problem related to the novel *Around the World in Eighty Days*, by Jules Verne. Read this example carefully. Then read the examples below.

**EXAMPLE A** | The wheel on Devin's unicycle has a diameter of 27 inches.

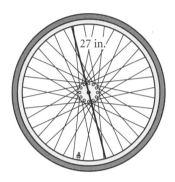

27 in.

    **a.** How far will the unicycle travel in 100 revolutions of the wheel? Give your answer to the nearest whole foot.

    **b.** Devin rides his unicycle 2 miles to school each day. About how many revolutions does the wheel make during his trip? (5280 feet = 1 mile)

▶ **Solution** | **a.** In one revolution, the wheel covers a distance equal to its circumference.

$$C = \pi d \qquad \text{The formula for circumference.}$$

$$C = \pi(27) \qquad \text{Substitute 27 for } d.$$

The unicycle travels $27\pi$ inches in one revolution. So, in 100 revolutions, it covers $(100) \cdot 27\pi \approx 8482$ inches, or about 707 feet.

    **b.** Two miles is 10,560 feet, or 126,720 inches. The wheel makes one revolution every $27\pi$ inches, so it makes $126{,}720 \div 27\pi$, or about 1494 revolutions during Devin's trip to school.

(continued)

**EXAMPLE B**  An audio CD spins at a rate of 200 rotations per minute. If the radius of a CD is 6 cm, how far does a point on the outer edge travel during the playing of a 57-minute CD?

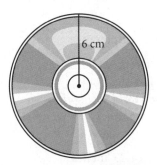

6 cm

▶ **Solution**  The point makes 200 rotations in 1 minute. So, in 57 minutes, it will make 200 · 57, or 11,400 rotations.

The distance the point travels in one rotation is equal to the circumference of the CD. Use the circumference formula to find this distance.

$C = 2\pi r$     The formula for circumference.

$C = 2\pi(6)$    Substitute 6 for $r$.

The point travels $12\pi$ cm in one rotation. So, in 11,400 rotations, it will travel 11,400 · $12\pi$, or 429,770 cm. This is equal to about 4.3 kilometers.

**EXAMPLE C**  The city of Rutledge wants to build a circular walking track that is a quarter-mile long. To keep vehicles off the track, the city plans to build a fence around the track. The fenced area will be square and the fence, at its closest point, will be 5 feet from the edge of the circular track. How many feet of fencing will be needed? Give your answer to the nearest foot and ignore any gates or openings. (1 mile = 5280 feet)

▶ **Solution**  Refer to the sketch at right.

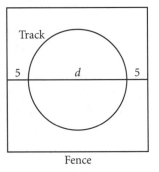

Track

5       $d$       5

Fence

First find the diameter of the track. The circumference of the track is 5280/4, or 1320 feet. Using $C = \pi d$, solve for $d$ to get $d = C/\pi$. So, $d = 1320/\pi$, or $d \approx 420.2$ feet. Each side of the square fence is 10 feet longer than the diameter of the track. Therefore, each side of the square must be about 430.2 feet. The amount of fencing needed is about 4 · 430.2 = 1720.8 feet, or to the nearest foot, 1721 feet.

# 6.7 Arc Length

In this lesson you will

- Learn the difference between **arc length** and **arc measure**
- Find a method for calculating arc length
- Solve problems involving arc length

In the figure at right, $\overarc{AB}$ and $\overarc{CD}$ have the same *measure* (45°) because their central angles, $\angle APB$ and $\angle CPD$, are the same angle. However, the *lengths* of $\overarc{AB}$ and $\overarc{CD}$ are clearly different—$\overarc{CD}$ is longer than $\overarc{AB}$. In this lesson you'll learn how to find the length of an arc.

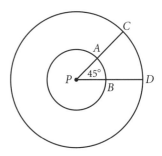

Read Example A in your book. It illustrates that if an arc has measure $x$, then the arc is $\frac{x}{360°}$ of the circle. For example, each of the 45° arcs in the figure at right is $\frac{45°}{360°}$, or $\frac{1}{8}$, of a complete circle.

Think about how the fractions in Example A are related to the length of the arc. If you travel a quarter of the way around a circle, you cover $\frac{1}{4}$ of its circumference. If you travel halfway around, you cover $\frac{1}{2}$ the circumference. The length of an arc, or **arc length,** is a fraction of the circumference of its circle. While arc measure is expressed in degrees, arc length is expressed in a unit of distance.

## Investigation: Finding the Arcs

Look at the figures in Step 1 in your book. Find the fraction of the circle each arc makes up. You should get the following results.

$\overarc{AB}$ is $\frac{1}{4}$ of circle $T$

$\overarc{CED}$ is $\frac{1}{2}$ of circle $O$

$\overarc{GH}$ is $\frac{140°}{360°}$, or $\frac{7}{18}$, of circle $P$

Now find the circumference of each circle using the formula $C = \pi d$ or $C = 2\pi r$. For example, because circle $P$ has radius 36 feet, its circumference is $2\pi(36)$, or $72\pi$ feet.

Use the fractions you found in Step 1 and the circumference of each circle to find the length of each arc. For example, $\overarc{GH}$ makes up $\frac{7}{18}$ of circle $P$, and circle $P$ has a circumference of $72\pi$. So,

Length of $\overarc{GH} = \frac{7}{18}(72\pi) = 28\pi$

The length of $\overarc{GH}$ is $28\pi$ feet.

Generalize this method for finding the length of an arc as a conjecture.

**Arc Length Conjecture** The length of an arc equals the circumference times the arc measure divided by _____. **C-66**

(continued)

**Lesson 6.7 • Arc Length (continued)**

Examples B and C in your book show how you can apply the Arc Length
Conjecture. Read these examples carefully. Then read the example below.

**EXAMPLE** | The length of $\overset{\frown}{SM}$ is $6\pi$ centimeters. What is the radius of circle $P$?

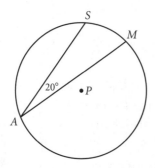

▶ **Solution** | $m\angle SAM = 20°$, so $m\overset{\frown}{SM} = 40°$ by the Inscribed Angle Conjecture. This means
that $\overset{\frown}{SM}$ is $\frac{40°}{360°}$, or $\frac{1}{9}$, of the circumference of the circle.

Arc length $\overset{\frown}{SM} = \frac{1}{9}C$    Use the Arc Length Conjecture.

$6\pi = \frac{1}{9}C$    Substitute $6\pi$ for the arc length.

$54\pi = C$    Multiply both sides by 9.

The circumference is $54\pi$ centimeters. Use the circumference formula to find
the radius.

$C = 2\pi r$    The circumference formula.

$54\pi = 2\pi r$    Substitute $7\pi$ for the arc length.

$27 = r$    Divide both sides by $2\pi$.

The radius is 27 centimeters.

*Discovering Geometry Condensed Lessons*
©2008 Key Curriculum Press

# 7.1 Transformations and Symmetry

In this lesson you will

- Learn about three types of **rigid transformations—translation, rotation,** and **reflection**
- Use patty paper to model reflection
- Learn how to identify figures with **rotational symmetry** or **reflectional symmetry**

In your book, read the text before the investigation. Below is a summary of some of the key points.

1. A transformation that creates an image that is congruent to the original figure is called a **rigid transformation,** or **isometry.** Three types of rigid transformations are **translation, rotation,** and **reflection.**

2. A transformation that changes the size or shape of a figure is a **nonrigid transformation.**

3. A **translation** slides a figure along a straight-line path, moving each point the same distance in the same direction. You can describe a translation using a **translation vector,** which specifies both the distance and the direction.

4. A **rotation** turns a figure about a fixed point, rotating each point the same number of degrees. You define a rotation by giving the center point, the number of degrees, and the direction (clockwise or counterclockwise). When a direction is not specified, the rotation is assumed to be counterclockwise.

5. A **reflection** flips a figure across a line, creating the mirror image of the figure. You define a reflection by specifying the **line of reflection.**

## Investigation: The Basic Property of a Reflection

Follow Steps 1 and 2 in your book to create a figure and its reflected image. Then draw segments connecting each vertex with its image point.

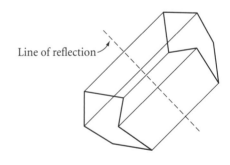

Line of reflection

Measure the angles where the segments intersect the line of reflection. What do you find? The line of reflection divides each connecting segment into two segments. How do the lengths of the two segments compare? Use your findings to complete this conjecture.

**Reflection Line Conjecture** The line of reflection is the _____ C-67 of every segment joining a point in the original figure with its image.

(continued)

Read the remaining text in this lesson. Below is a summary of the key points.

1. A figure that can be reflected across a line so that the resulting image coincides with the original has **reflectional symmetry.** The reflection line is called a **line of symmetry.** A figure can have more than one line of symmetry. A figure with *n* lines of symmetry has *n*-fold reflectional symmetry.

2. A figure that can be rotated *less than a full turn* about a point so that the rotated image coincides with the original has **rotational symmetry.** If the image coincides with the original figure *n* times during a full turn, then the figure is said to have *n*-fold rotational symmetry. A figure that has 2-fold rotational symmetry is also said to have **point symmetry.**

**EXAMPLE** | Describe all the symmetries of an equilateral triangle.

▶ **Solution** | An equilateral triangle has three reflectional symmetries. There is a line of reflection through each vertex and the midpoint of the opposite side.

An equilateral triangle has three rotational symmetries (that is, it has 3-fold rotational symmetry). It can be rotated 120°, 240°, and 360° about its center, and it will coincide with itself.

# 7.2 Properties of Isometries

In this lesson you will

- Use **ordered pair rules** to transform polygons in the coordinate plane
- Learn the ordered pair rules that correspond to various **isometries**
- Discover how to determine the **minimal path** from a point to a line to another point on the same side of the line

You can use an ordered pair rule to transform figures in the coordinate plane. An **ordered pair rule** describes how each point in an original figure is relocated to create an image.

Example A in your book illustrates that the rule $(x, y) \rightarrow (x + 2, y - 3)$ is a translation that moves each point of a figure right 2 units and down 3 units. The translation vector is written $\langle 2, -3 \rangle$. Read Example A. In general, the rule $(x, y) \rightarrow (x + h, y + k)$ is a translation of $h$ units horizontally and $k$ units vertically. The general translation vector is written $\langle h, k \rangle$.

## Investigation 1: Transformations on a Coordinate Plane

In this investigation you will explore four ordered pair rules.

Follow Steps 1 and 2 in your book. Draw your original polygon in Quadrant I, II, or IV. (Here are some examples in which the original polygon is in Quadrant III.)

Using your drawings and some patty paper, determine whether each transformation is a reflection, translation, or rotation. Identify the lines of reflection and centers and angles of rotation.

Now consider the examples. In each graph, the solid figure in Quadrant III is the original, and the dashed figure is the image. (*Note:* The line $y = x$ has been added to the last graph.) Determine how the original figure has been transformed to create the image. Do you get the same results you got for your polygon?

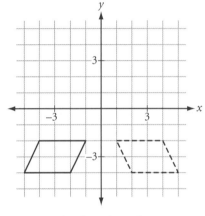

$(x, y) \rightarrow (-x, y)$

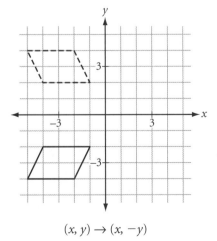

$(x, y) \rightarrow (x, -y)$

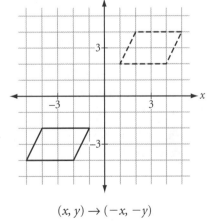

$(x, y) \rightarrow (-x, -y)$

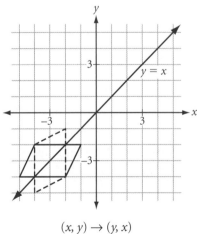

$(x, y) \rightarrow (y, x)$

(continued)

Use your findings to complete the Coordinate Transformations Conjecture in your book.

Now you will revisit "poolroom geometry." Recall that when a ball rolls without spin into a cushion, the outgoing angle is congruent to the incoming angle.

## Investigation 2: Finding a Minimal Path

Follow Steps 1–4 of the investigation in your book. Then unfold the paper and draw $\overline{AB'}$. Notice that $\overline{AB'}$ passes through point $C$.

Measure the length of the path from $A$ to $B'$. Measure the length of the two-part path from $A$ to $C$ to $B$. You should find that the lengths of the paths are the same.

The path from $A$ to $C$ to $B$ is the shortest path, or the **minimal path,** from $A$ to the cushion to $B$. To see why, choose any other point $D$ on the cushion. The path from $A$ to $D$ to $B$ is the same length as the path from $A$ to $D$ to $B'$. $\overline{AB'}$ is shorter than the path from $A$ to $D$ to $B'$ (why?), so it is also shorter than the path from $A$ to $D$ to $B$. Because $\overline{AB'}$ is the same length as the path from $A$ to $C$ to $B$, the path from $A$ to $C$ to $B$ is shorter than the path from $A$ to $D$ to $B$. This argument is given in symbols below.

$AD + DB = AD + DB'$

$\qquad AB' < AD + DB'$

$\qquad AB' < AD + DB$

$\qquad AB' = AC + CB$

$AC + CB < AD + DB$

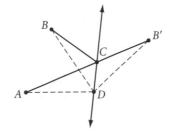

Complete this conjecture.

---

**Minimal Path Conjecture** If points $A$ and $B$ are on one side of line $\ell$, then | **C-69**
the minimal path from point $A$ to line $\ell$ to point $B$ is found by reflecting
point _____ across line $\ell$, drawing segment _____,
then drawing segments $AC$ and _____, where point $C$ is the
point of intersection of segment _____ and line $\ell$.

---

Your findings in the investigation show that if you want to hit a ball from point $A$ off the cushion so it passes through point $B$, you should visualize point $B$ reflected across the cushion and then aim at the reflected image.

Example B in your book applies what you learned in Investigation 2 to solve a problem about miniature golf. Read this example.

# 7.3 Compositions of Transformations

In this lesson you will

- Find the single transformation equivalent to the **composition of two translations**
- Find the single transformation equivalent to the **composition of reflections across two parallel lines**
- Find the single transformation equivalent to the **composition of reflections across two intersecting lines**

When you apply a transformation to a figure and then apply another transformation to its image, the resulting transformation is called a **composition** of transformations.

In the example in your book, a figure is translated by one rule and then its image is translated by a different rule. The composition of the two translations is equivalent to a single translation. Read this example carefully and make sure you understand it.

## Investigation 1: Reflections across Two Parallel Lines

Follow Steps 1–4 to reflect a figure across one line and then reflect the image across a second line, parallel to the first.

What single transformation would take the original figure to the final image? (*Hint:* How does the orientation of the final image compare with the orientation of the original?)

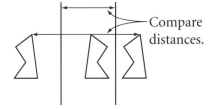

Compare distances.

Use a compass or patty paper to compare the distance between the parallel lines to the distance between a point on the original figure and the corresponding point on the final image.

Use your findings to complete this conjecture.

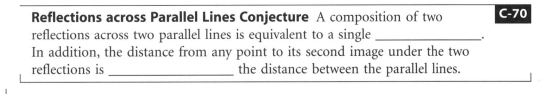

**Reflections across Parallel Lines Conjecture** A composition of two reflections across two parallel lines is equivalent to a single _____. In addition, the distance from any point to its second image under the two reflections is _____ the distance between the parallel lines.

C-70

Read the example on the next page.

(continued)

**EXAMPLE** | Lines *m* and *n* are parallel and 13 cm apart.

a. Point *A* is 4 cm from line *m* and 17 cm from line *n*. Point *A* is reflected across line *m*, and then its image, *A′*, is reflected across line *n* to create a second image, point *A″*. How far is point *A* from point *A″*?

b. What if *A* is reflected across *n*, and then its image is reflected across *m*? Find the new image and distance.

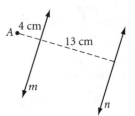

▶ **Solution** | a. By the Reflections across Parallel Lines Conjecture, the distance between *A* and *A″* is 26 cm, twice the distance between the lines. A drawing verifies this.

b. By the Reflections across Parallel Lines Conjecture, the distance between *A* and *A″* is 26 cm. A drawing verifies this.

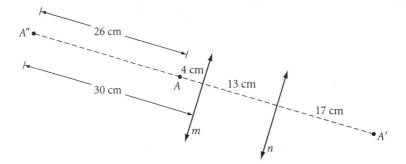

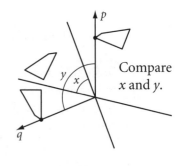

## Investigation 2: Reflections across Two Intersecting Lines

Follow Steps 1–4 to reflect a figure across one line and then reflect the image across a second line that intersects the first.

Draw two rays, *p* and *q*, that start at the point of intersection of the two lines and that pass through corresponding points on the original figure and its second image. What single transformation would take the original figure to the final image?

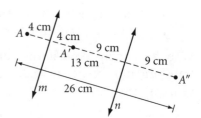

You should have found that the two reflections are equivalent to a single rotation. Use a protractor to compare the angle of rotation (that is, the angle created by rays *p* and *q*) with the acute angle formed by the intersecting lines. Use your findings to complete this conjecture.

**Reflections across Intersecting Lines Conjecture** A composition of two reflections across a pair of intersecting lines is equivalent to a single _____. The angle of _____ is _____ the acute angle between the pair of intersecting reflection lines.     **C-71**

There are many other ways to combine transformations. For example, the composition of a translation and a reflection is called a **glide reflection.** Page 386 of your book shows examples of glide reflection.

# Tessellations with Regular Polygons

**CONDENSED**
**LESSON**
**7.4**

In this lesson you will

- Learn about the three **regular tessellations**
- Discover all the possible **semiregular tessellations**

An arrangement of shapes that covers a plane completely without gaps or overlaps is called a **tessellation** or **tiling.** Read the text in your book before the investigation. Here is a summary of the main points.

1. For shapes to create a tessellation, their angles, when arranged around a point, must have measures that add to exactly 360°.

2. A tiling that uses only one shape is called a **monohedral tessellation.**

3. A monohedral tessellation of congruent regular polygons is called a **regular tessellation.** The only polygons that create a regular tessellation are equilateral triangles, squares, and regular hexagons. (These are the regular polygons with angle measures that are factors of 360°.)

4. When the same combination of two or more regular polygons meet in the same order at each vertex of a tessellation, it is called a **semiregular tessellation.**

5. You can describe a tessellation by giving its **vertex arrangement,** or **numerical name.** To name a tessellation, list the number of sides of each shape, in order as you move around a vertex. For example, each vertex of the tessellation at right is surrounded by a square (4 sides), a hexagon (6 sides), and a dodecagon (12 sides). So, the numerical name for this tessellation is 4.6.12.

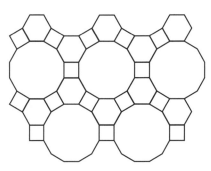

## Investigation: The Semiregular Tessellations

There are eight different semiregular tessellations. Your book shows three (4.8.8, or 4.8², 4.6.12, and 3.12.12, or 3.12²). In this investigation you will find the other five. All five are made from combinations of triangles, squares, and hexagons.

You will need triangles, squares, and hexagons either from a set of pattern blocks or traced or copied from the set below and cut out. If you have geometry software available, you may use that instead.

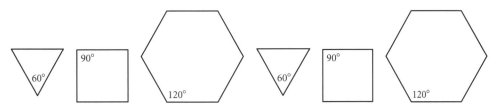

First, look for combinations of *two* polygons that can be used to create a semiregular tessellation. Start by finding combinations of angle measures that add to 360°. For example, because 4 · 60° + 120° = 360°, four triangles and one hexagon could be arranged around a vertex. Try to find a way to arrange the shapes so the pattern can be continued indefinitely. (Remember, the polygons must meet in the *same order* at each vertex.)

(continued)

Here is the tessellation, labeled with its numerical name.

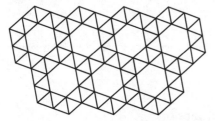

3.3.3.3.6 or $3^4.6$

Find the remaining four semiregular tessellations that can be made with two different polygons. Sketch each one and label it with its numerical name.

Now look for combinations of *three* polygons that can be used to create semiregular tessellations. Again, first find combinations of angle measures that add to 360°, and then make the tessellation. Find at least one semiregular tessellation that can be made with three different polgyons. Sketch it and label it with its numerical name.

Read the remaining text in this lesson. Here is a summary of the key points.

1. The three regular and eight semiregular tessellations are called the **Archimedean tilings.**

2. The regular and semiregular tessellations are also called *1-uniform tilings* because all the vertices are identical. A tessellation with two types of vertices is called *2-uniform,* a tessellation with three types of vertices is called *3-uniform,* and so on. (See the illustrations in your book for examples.)

*Discovering Geometry Condensed Lessons*
©2008 Key Curriculum Press

# Tessellations with Nonregular Polygons

CONDENSED
LESSON
7.5

In this lesson you will

- Determine whether all triangles tessellate
- Determine whether all quadrilaterals tessellate
- Look at some examples of pentagonal tessellations

In Lesson 7.4, you investigated tessellations that were formed from regular polygons. Now you will try to create tessellations from nonregular polygons.

## Investigation 1: Do All Triangles Tessellate?

Follow the steps for "Making Congruent Triangles" on page 394 in your book to create and label 12 congruent scalene triangles. Try to form a tessellation using the triangles. Here is an example.

Look at your tessellation and the tessellation below. You should find that, in both tessellations, each angle fits twice around each vertex point.

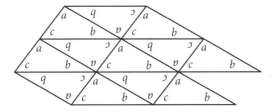

The sum of the measures of the angles of a triangle is 180°. Because each angle fits twice around each point, the sum of the measures of the angles around each point is 2(180°), or 360°. As you saw in Lesson 7.4, this is the sum of the angles surrounding each vertex in *any* tessellation.

Do you think you would be able to create a tessellation using an isosceles triangle? Try it and see.

Your findings from this investigation lead to the following conjecture.

> **Tessellating Triangles Conjecture** Any triangle will create a monohedral tessellation.
>
> **C-72**

You know that squares and rectangles can tile a plane, and you can probably visualize tiling with parallelograms. Will any quadrilateral tessellate? You will explore this question in the next investigation.

(continued)

## Investigation 2: Do All Quadrilaterals Tessellate?

Create 12 congruent quadrilaterals (not parallelograms or trapezoids), and label the corresponding angles in each quadrilateral *a*, *b*, *c*, and *d*. Try to form a tessellation using the quadrilaterals. Here is an example.

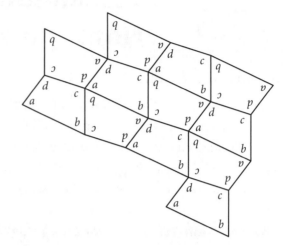

Look at your tessellation and the tessellation at right. You should find that, in both tessellations, each angle fits once around each vertex point. This makes sense because the sum of the angle measures of a quadrilateral is 360°. Your findings lead to this conjecture.

> **Tessellating Quadrilaterals Conjecture** Any quadrilateral will create a monohedral tessellation.
>
> **C-73**

You know that a regular pentagon will not tessellate. However, it is possible to create tessellations from other types of pentagons. Pages 395 and 396 of your book show some examples. So far, 14 types of pentagons have been shown to tessellate. No one currently knows if there are more.

In the next example, you will create a pentagonal tessellation. This example is Exercise 2 in your book. Refer to Exercises 9 and 10 in Lesson 7.4 for a description of *dual* tessellations.

**EXAMPLE** | Produce a pentagonal tessellation by creating the *dual* of the semiregular tessellation at right.

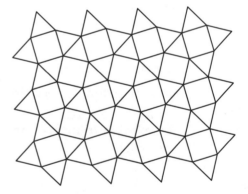

▶ **Solution** | Recall that the dual is created by connecting the centers of the polygons that surround each vertex point. Here is the result.

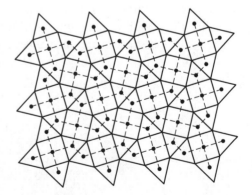

# Areas of Rectangles and Parallelograms

In this lesson you will

- Review the formula for the area of a rectangle
- Use the area formula for rectangles to find areas of other shapes
- Discover the formula for the area of a parallelogram

The **area** of a plane figure is the number of square units that can be arranged to fill the figure completely.

You probably already know several area formulas. The investigations in this chapter will help you understand and remember the formulas.

Pages 422 and 423 of your book discuss the formula for the area of a rectangle. Read this text carefully. Make sure

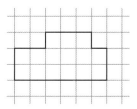

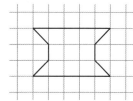

Area = 15 square units          Area = 11 square units

that you understand the meaning of **base** and **height** and that the area formula makes sense to you, then complete the Rectangle Area Conjecture in your book. Example A in your book shows how the area formula for rectangles can help you find areas of other shapes. Here is another example.

**EXAMPLE A**    Find the area of this square.

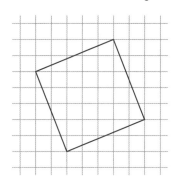

▶ **Solution**    Surround the given "slanted" square with a 7-by-7 square with horizontal and vertical sides. Then subtract the area of the four right triangles formed from the area of the surrounding square.

Each of the four triangles is half of a 2-by-5 rectangle, so each has area $\frac{1}{2} \cdot 2 \cdot 5$, or 5 square units. Therefore, the area of the original square is $(7 \cdot 7) - (4 \cdot 5) = 29$ square units.

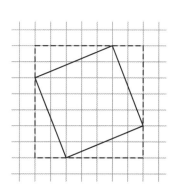

(continued)

## Lesson 8.1 • Areas of Rectangles and Parallelograms (continued)

Just as with a rectangle, any side of a parallelogram can be called the *base*. An **altitude** of a parallelogram is any segment from one side of the parallelogram, perpendicular to that side, to a line through the opposite side. The *height* of a parallelogram is the length of the altitude. Study the diagrams of altitudes on page 424 of your book.

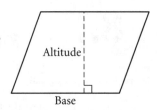

### Investigation: Area Formula for Parallelograms

Follow Steps 1 and 2 of the investigation in your book. In Step 2, each new shape you form has the same area as the original parallelogram because you have simply rearranged pieces, without adding or removing any cardboard.

Form a rectangle with the two pieces.

Notice that the base and height of the rectangle are the same as the base and height of the original parallelogram. Because the area of the rectangle and the parallelogram are the same, the area of the parallelogram is *bh*. This can be summarized as a conjecture.

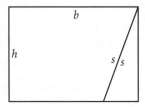

> **Parallelogram Area Conjecture** The area of a parallelogram is given by the **C-75** formula $A = bh$, where $A$ is the area, $b$ is the length of the base, and $h$ is the height of the parallelogram.

If the dimensions of a figure are measured in inches, feet, or yards, the area is measured in $in^2$ (square inches), $ft^2$ (square feet), or $yd^2$ (square yards). If the dimensions are measured in centimeters or meters, the area is measured in $cm^2$ (square centimeters) or $m^2$ (square meters). Read Example B in your book, and then read the example below.

**EXAMPLE B** | A parallelogram has height 5.6 ft and area 70 $ft^2$. Find the length of the base.

▶ **Solution** |

$A = bh$      Write the formula.

$70 = b(5.6)$      Substitute the known values.

$\dfrac{70}{5.6} = b$      Solve for the base length.

$12.5 = b$      Divide.

The length of the base is 12.5 ft.

*Discovering Geometry Condensed Lessons*
©2008 Key Curriculum Press

# Areas of Triangles, Trapezoids, and Kites

In this lesson you will

- Discover area formulas for triangles, trapezoids, and kites

You can use the area formulas you already know to derive new area formulas. In the first investigation you will focus on triangles.

### Investigation 1: Area Formula for Triangles

Follow Step 1 in your book to create and label a pair of congruent triangles.

You know the area formula for rectangles and parallelograms. Arrange the two congruent triangles to form one of these figures. Write an expression for the area of the entire figure. Then write an expression for the area of one of the triangles.

Summarize your findings by completing the conjecture below.

**Triangle Area Conjecture** The area of a triangle is given by the formula _____, where $A$ is the area, $b$ is the length of the base, and $h$ is the height of the triangle. **C-76**

Next, you'll consider the area of a trapezoid.

### Investigation 2: Area Formula for Trapezoids

Follow Steps 1 and 2 in your book to make and label two congruent trapezoids. You can arrange the trapezoids to form a parallelogram.

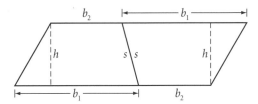

What is the base length of the parallelogram? What is the height? Use your answers to the questions to write an expression for the area of the parallelogram. Then use the expression for the area of the parallelogram to write an expression for the area of one trapezoid.

Summarize your findings by completing this conjecture.

**Trapezoid Area Conjecture** The area of a trapezoid is given by the formula _____, where $A$ is the area, $b_1$ and $b_2$ are the lengths of the two bases, and $h$ is the height of the trapezoid. **C-77**

(continued)

Finally, you will consider the area of a kite.

## Investigation 3: Area Formula for Kites

Draw a kite. Draw its diagonals. Let $d_1$ be the length of the diagonal connecting the vertex angles, and let $d_2$ be the length of the other diagonal.

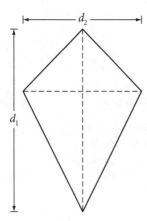

Recall that the diagonal connecting the vertex angles of a kite divides it into two congruent triangles. Consider the diagonal labeled $d_1$ to be the base of one of the triangles. Then, because the diagonal connecting the vertex angles of a kite is the perpendicular bisector of the other diagonal, the height of the triangle is $\frac{1}{2}d_2$.

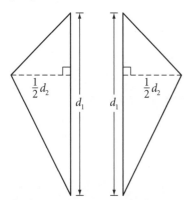

Write an expression for the area of one of the triangles. Then use the expression for the area of the triangle to write an expression for the area of the kite.

Summarize your findings by completing this conjecture.

---

**Kite Area Conjecture** The area of a kite is given by the formula         , where $A$ is the area and $d_1$ and $d_2$ are the lengths of the diagonals.

**C-78**

---

# 8.3 Area Problems

In this lesson you will

- Use a variety of strategies to approximate the areas of irregularly shaped figures
- Use the area formulas from the previous two lessons to find the areas of more complex figures

You have discovered formulas for areas of rectangles, parallelograms, triangles, trapezoids, and kites. In this lesson you will use these formulas, along with other methods, to find the approximate areas of irregularly shaped figures.

## Investigation: Solving Problems with Area Formulas

On the next page, you'll find eight geometric figures. For each figure, find a way to calculate the approximate area. Then record the area and write a sentence or two explaining how you found it. It may help to trace a figure onto another sheet of paper.

Below are some hints for how you might find the area of each figure. Read these hints only if you get stuck. There are lots of ways to find each area. The methods you use may be very different from those described here.

**Figure A**   Divide the figure into rectangles.

**Figure B**   This figure is a kite. Use what you learned in Lesson 8.2 to find the area.

**Figure C**   This figure is a parallelogram. Use what you learned in Lesson 8.1 to find the area.

**Figure D**   Divide the figure into triangles.

**Figure E**   This figure is a trapezoid. Use what you learned in Lesson 8.2 to find the area.

**Figure F**   Find the area of the two squares. Cut out the other two pieces and rearrange them to form a recognizable shape.

**Figure G**   Divide this dodecagon into 12 identical, isosceles triangles with vertex angles at the "center" of the polygon.

**Figure H**   Trace the figure onto a sheet of graph paper. Estimate the number of squares that fit inside the figure. Or draw as large a rectangle as will fit in the shape. Cut off the remaining pieces and arrange them to form recognizable shapes.

(continued)

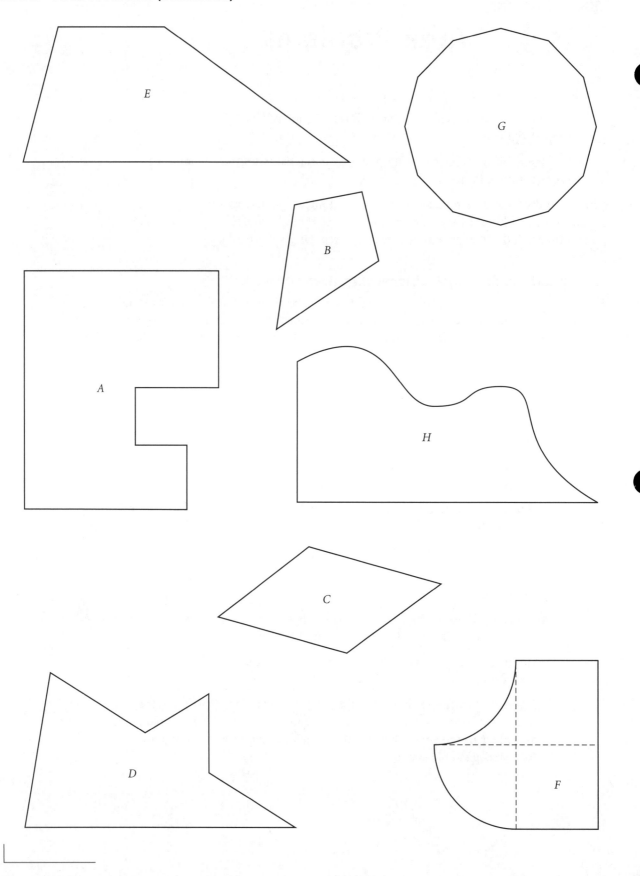

# 8.4 Areas of Regular Polygons

In this lesson you will

- Discover the area formula for regular polygons

You can divide a regular polygon into congruent isosceles triangles by drawing segments from the center of the polygon to each vertex. The center of the polygon is actually the center of the circumscribed circle, so each of these congruent segments is called a radius of the regular polygon.

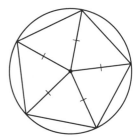

In the investigation you will divide regular polygons into triangles. Then you will write a formula for the area of any regular polygon.

### Investigation: Area Formula for Regular Polygons

The **apothem** of a regular polygon is a perpendicular segment from the center of the polygon's circumscribed circle to a side of the polygon. The apothem is also the length of the segment. Follow the steps in your book to find the formula for the area of a regular $n$-sided polygon with sides of length $s$ and apothem $a$. Your findings can be summarized in this conjecture.

> **Regular Polygon Area Conjecture** The area of a regular polygon is given **C-79** by the formula $A = \frac{1}{2}asn$ or $A = \frac{1}{2}aP$, where $A$ is the area, $P$ is the perimeter, $a$ is the apothem, $s$ is the length of each side, and $n$ is the number of sides.

The examples below show you how to apply your new formulas.

**EXAMPLE A** | The area of a regular nonagon is about 302.4 cm² and the apothem is about 9.6 cm. Find the approximate length of each side.

▶ **Solution** | Because you are trying to find the side length, $s$, it is probably easier to use the formula $A = \frac{1}{2}asn$. You could also use $A = \frac{1}{2}aP$, solve for $P$, and then divide the result by 9 (the number of sides).

$A = \frac{1}{2}asn$      Write the formula.

$302.4 \approx \frac{1}{2}(9.6)(s)(9)$    Substitute the known values.

$302.4 \approx 43.2s$      Multiply.

$\frac{302.4}{43.2} \approx s$      Solve for $s$.

$7 \approx s$      Divide.

Each side is about 7 cm long.

(continued)

**EXAMPLE B**  Find the shaded area of the regular pentagon *PENTA*. The apothem measures about 2.0 cm. Segment *PE* measures about 2.9 cm.

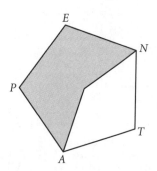

▶ **Solution**  First, find the area of the entire pentagon.

$A = \frac{1}{2}asn$        Write the formula.

$A \approx \frac{1}{2}(2.0)(2.9)(5)$        Substitute the known values.

$A \approx 14.5$        Multiply.

The area of the pentagon is about 14.5 cm². The shaded portion makes up $\frac{3}{5}$ of the pentagon. (If you divide the pentagon into five isosceles triangles, three will be shaded.) So, the shaded area is about $\frac{3}{5} \cdot 14.5$ cm², or 8.7 cm².

# 8.5 Areas of Circles

In this lesson you will

- Discover the area formula for circles

A rectangle has straight sides, while a circle is entirely curved. So, it may surprise you that you can use the area formula for rectangles to help you find the area formula for circles. In the next investigation you'll see how.

## Investigation: Area Formula for Circles

Follow Steps 1–3 in your book to create a figure like the one below.

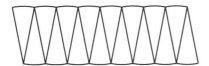

The figure resembles a parallelogram with two bumpy sides. If you cut the circle into more wedges, you could arrange these thinner wedges to look more like a rectangle. You would not lose or gain any area in this change, so the area of this new "rectangle" would be the same as the area of the original circle. If you could cut infinitely many wedges, you'd actually have a rectangle with smooth sides.

The two longer sides of the rectangle would be made up of the circumference, $C$, of the circle. (Each side would be half the circumference.) Consider one of these sides to be the base. Recall the formula for the circumference of a circle that you learned in Chapter 6. Now use this formula to write the length of the base of the rectangle in terms of $r$, the radius of the original circle.

How is the height of the rectangle related to the original circle?

Remember, the area of the rectangle is the same as the area of the original circle. Use this idea and your findings to complete this conjecture.

> **Circle Area Conjecture** The area of a circle is given by the formula **C-80**
> $A =$ _____, where $A$ is the area and $r$ is the radius of the circle.

Examples A and B in your book show how to use your new conjecture. Read these examples, and then read the examples on the next page.

(continued)

**EXAMPLE A** | The circumference of a circle is $22\pi$ ft. What is the area of the circle?

▶ **Solution** | Use the circumference formula to find the radius. Then use the area formula to find the area.

$C = 2\pi r$ — Write the formula for circumference.

$22\pi = 2\pi r$ — Substitute the known values.

$11 = r$ — Solve for $r$.

$A = \pi r^2$ — Write the formula for area.

$A = \pi(11)^2$ — Substitute the known values.

$A = 121\pi$ — Simplify.

The area is $121\pi$ ft$^2$, or about 380.1 ft$^2$.

**EXAMPLE B** | At Maria's Pizzeria, a pepperoni pizza with diameter 10 inches costs $8, and a pepperoni pizza with diameter 12 inches costs $10. Which size is a better buy?

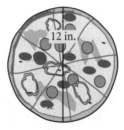

$8                    $10

▶ **Solution** | Find the area of each pizza, and then find the price per square inch.

**10-inch pizza**

$A = \pi r^2$

$= \pi(5)^2$

$= 25\pi$

The area is $25\pi$ in$^2$. To find the cost per square inch, divide the price by the area.

$\dfrac{8}{25\pi} \approx 0.10$

The 10-inch pizza costs about 10¢ per square inch.

**12-inch pizza**

$A = \pi r^2$

$= \pi(6)^2$

$= 36\pi$

The area is $36\pi$ in$^2$. To find the cost per square inch, divide the price by the area.

$\dfrac{10}{36\pi} \approx 0.09$

The 12-inch pizza costs about 9¢ per square inch.

The 12-inch pizza costs less per square inch, so the 12-inch pizza is a better buy.

# 8.6   Any Way You Slice It

In this lesson you will

- Learn how to find the area of a sector, a segment, and an annulus of a circle

In Lesson 8.5, you discovered the formula for calculating the area of a circle. In this lesson you'll learn how to find the areas of three types of sections of a circle.

A **sector of a circle** is the region between two radii and an arc of the circle.

A **segment of a circle** is the region between a chord and an arc of the circle.

An **annulus** is the region between two concentric circles.

Examples of the three types of sections are pictured below.

| Sector of a circle | Segment of a circle | Annulus |

The "picture equations" below show you how to calculate the area of each type of section.

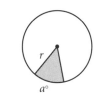   

$$\frac{a}{360} \cdot \pi r^2 = A_{\text{sector}}$$        $$\frac{a}{360}\pi r^2 - \frac{1}{2}bh = A_{\text{segment}}$$        $$\pi R^2 - \pi r^2 = A_{\text{annulus}}$$

Read the examples in your book carefully. Then read the examples below.

**EXAMPLE A**   $R = 9$ cm and $r = 3$ cm. Find the area of the annulus.

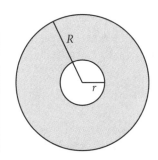

(continued)

▶ **Solution**

$A = \pi R^2 - \pi r^2$    The area formula for an annulus.

$= \pi(9)^2 - \pi(3)^2$    Substitute the values for $R$ and $r$.

$= 81\pi - 9\pi$    Evaluate the exponents.

$= 72\pi$    Subtract.

The area of the annulus is $72\pi$ cm², or about 226 cm².

**EXAMPLE B**    The shaded area is $21\pi$ cm². The radius of the large circle is 12 cm, and the radius of the small circle is 9 cm. Find $x$, the measure of the central angle.

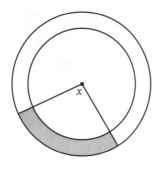

▶ **Solution**    First, find the area of the whole annulus.

$A = \pi R^2 - \pi r^2$    The area formula for an annulus.

$= \pi(12)^2 - \pi(9)^2$    Substitute the values for $R$ and $r$.

$= 63\pi$    Simplify.

The shaded area, $21\pi$ cm², is $\frac{x}{360}$ of the area of the annulus. Use this information to write and solve an equation.

$$21\pi = \frac{x}{360} \cdot 63\pi$$

$$360 \cdot \frac{21\pi}{63\pi} = x$$

$$120 = x$$

The measure of the central angle is 120°.

# Surface Area

In this lesson you will

- Learn how to find the surface areas of prisms, pyramids, cylinders, and cones

You can use what you know about finding the areas of plane figures to find the surface areas of prisms, pyramids, cylinders, and cones. The **surface area** of each of these solids is the sum of the areas of all the faces or surfaces that enclose the solid. The faces include the solid's **bases** and its **lateral faces.**

In a prism, the bases are two congruent polygons and the lateral faces are rectangles or other parallelograms. In a pyramid, the base can be any polygon and the lateral faces are triangles.

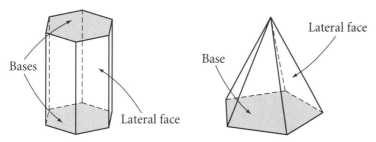

Read the "Steps for Finding Surface Area" on page 462 of your book. Example A shows how to find the surface area of a rectangular prism. Read the example carefully.

Then read Example B, which shows how to find the surface area of a cylinder. Notice that, to find the area of the cylinder's lateral surface, you need to imagine cutting the surface and laying it flat to get a rectangle. Because the rectangle wraps exactly around the circular base, the length of the rectangle's base is the circumference of the circular base.

The surface area of a pyramid is the area of the base, plus the areas of the triangular faces. The height of each triangular face is called the **slant height.** Use $l$ for the slant height and $h$ for the height of the pyramid.

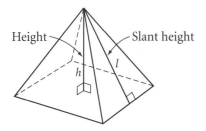

Height — — Slant height

$h$   $l$

(continued)

### Investigation 1: Surface Area of a Regular Pyramid

The lateral faces of a regular pyramid are identical isosceles triangles, and the base is a regular polygon.

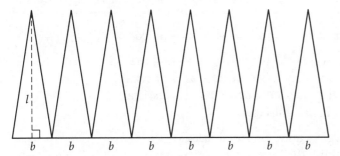 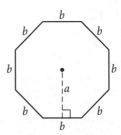

Each lateral face is a triangle with base length $b$ and height $l$. What is the area of each face?

If the base is an $n$-gon, then there are $n$ lateral faces. What is the total lateral surface area of the pyramid?

What is the area of the base in terms of $a$, $b$, and $n$?

Use your expressions to write a formula for the surface area of a regular $n$-gon pyramid in terms of the number of sides $n$, base length $b$, slant height $l$, and apothem $a$.

Using the fact that the perimeter of the base is $nb$, write another formula for the surface area of a regular $n$-gon pyramid in terms of slant height $l$, apothem $a$, and perimeter of the base, $P$.

In the next investigation you will find the surface area of a cone with radius $r$ and slant height $l$.

### Investigation 2: Surface Area of a Cone

As the number of faces of a pyramid increases, it begins to look like a cone. You can think of the lateral surface as many thin triangles or as a sector of a circle. You can rearrange the triangles to form a rectangle.

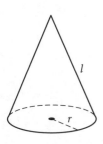 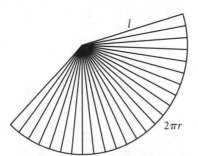 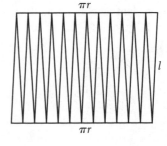

Use the diagrams to help you write a formula for the lateral surface area in terms of $r$ and $l$.

Using the expression for the lateral surface area and an expression for the area of the base, write a formula for the surface area of the cone.

(continued)

**Lesson 8.7 • Surface Area (continued)**

Example C in your book shows you how to apply the formula for the surface area
of a cone. Read Example C carefully. Then read the example below.

**EXAMPLE** | Find the surface area of this solid. $D = 10$, $d = 6$, $h = 14$.

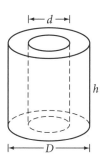

▶ **Solution** | The surface area is the lateral surface area of the outside cylinder, plus the
lateral surface area of the inside cylinder, plus the area of the two bases, which
are annuluses.

$$\text{Lateral surface area of outside cylinder} = 2\pi\left(\frac{D}{2}\right)h = 2\pi\left(\frac{10}{2}\right)(14) = 140\pi \text{ cm}^2$$

$$\text{Lateral surface area of inside cylinder} = 2\pi\left(\frac{d}{2}\right)h = 2\pi\left(\frac{6}{2}\right)(14) = 84\pi \text{ cm}^2$$

$$\text{Area of one base} = \pi\left(\frac{D}{2}\right)^2 - \pi\left(\frac{d}{2}\right)^2$$

$$= \pi\left(\frac{10}{2}\right)^2 - \pi\left(\frac{6}{2}\right)^2 = 16\pi \text{ cm}^2$$

So,

Total surface area $= 140\pi + 84\pi + 2(16\pi) = 256\pi \text{ cm}^2 \approx 804 \text{ cm}^2$.

# The Theorem of Pythagoras

In this lesson you will

- Learn about the **Pythagorean Theorem,** which states the relationship between the lengths of the legs and the length of the hypotenuse of a right triangle
- Solve a **dissection puzzle** that helps you understand the Pythagorean Theorem
- Read a **proof** of the Pythagorean Theorem
- Use the Pythagorean Theorem to **solve problems**

In a right triangle, the side opposite the right angle is called the **hypotenuse** and the other sides are called **legs.** In the figure, $a$ and $b$ are the lengths of the legs of a right triangle, and $c$ is the length of the hypotenuse. There is a special relationship between the lengths of the legs and the length of the hypotenuse. This relationship is known as the Pythagorean Theorem.

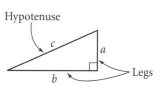

## Investigation: The Three Sides of a Right Triangle

In this investigation you will solve a geometric puzzle that will help you understand the Pythagorean Theorem. You will use a **dissection,** cutting apart a figure and putting the pieces back together to form a new figure.

Construct a scalene right triangle in the middle of a piece of paper. Label the two legs $a$ and $b$, and label the hypotenuse $c$. Construct a square on each side of the triangle so that the squares do not overlap the triangle. What is the area of each square in terms of its side length?

Now follow Steps 2–4 in your book.

After you successfully solve the puzzle in Step 4, explain the relationship among the areas of the three squares. Then use this relationship to complete the statement of the Pythagorean Theorem.

**The Pythagorean Theorem** In a right triangle, the sum of the squares of     **C-81**
the lengths of the legs equals _____.

If $a$ and $b$ are the lengths of the two legs of a right triangle and $c$ is the length of the hypotenuse, then a convenient way to write the Pythagorean Theorem is $a^2 + b^2 = c^2$.

A **theorem** is a conjecture that has been proved. There are over 200 known proofs of the Pythagorean Theorem. Your book gives one proof. Read the proof on page 479 of your book and make sure you can explain each step.

(continued)

## Lesson 9.1 • The Theorem of Pythagoras (continued)

Page 480 of your book gives some examples that illustrate that the Pythagorean relationship, $a^2 + b^2 = c^2$, does not hold for acute or obtuse triangles.

You can use the Pythagorean Theorem to solve problems involving right triangles. Read Examples A and B in your book, and then read the examples below.

**EXAMPLE A**  An Olympic soccer field is a rectangle 100 meters long and 70 meters wide. How long is the diagonal of the field?

▶ **Solution**  The diagonal is the hypotenuse of a right triangle with leg lengths 70 m and 100 m. You can use the Pythagorean Theorem to find its length.

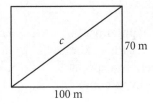

$$a^2 + b^2 = c^2 \qquad \text{The Pythagorean formula.}$$

$$70^2 + 100^2 = c^2 \qquad \text{Substitute the known values.}$$

$$4{,}900 + 10{,}000 = c^2 \qquad \text{Square the terms.}$$

$$14{,}900 = c^2 \qquad \text{Add.}$$

$$122 \approx c \qquad \text{Take the positive square root of each side.}$$

The diagonal is about 122 meters long.

**EXAMPLE B**  What is the area of a right triangle with a leg of length 5 feet and a hypotenuse of length 13 feet?

▶ **Solution**  You can consider the two legs to be the base and the height of the triangle. The length of one leg is 5 feet. To find the length of the other leg, use the Pythagorean Theorem.

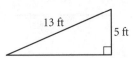

$$a^2 + b^2 = c^2 \qquad \text{The Pythagorean formula.}$$

$$5^2 + b^2 = 13^2 \qquad \text{Substitute.}$$

$$25 + b^2 = 169 \qquad \text{Square the terms.}$$

$$b^2 = 144 \qquad \text{Subtract 25 from both sides.}$$

$$b = 12 \qquad \text{Take the positive square root of each side.}$$

The other leg has length 12, so the area is $\frac{1}{2} \cdot 5 \cdot 12$, or 30 square feet.

*Discovering Geometry Condensed Lessons*
©2008 Key Curriculum Press

# The Converse of the Pythagorean Theorem

In this lesson you will

- Experiment with **Pythagorean triples** to determine whether the converse of the Pythagorean Theorem appears to be true
- Prove the **Converse of the Pythagorean Theorem**
- Use the converse of the Pythagorean Theorem to determine whether a triangle is a right triangle

In Lesson 9.1, you learned the Pythagorean Theorem, which states that if a triangle is a right triangle, then the square of the length of its hypotenuse is equal to the sum of the squares of the lengths of the two legs. Do you think the converse is also true? In other words, if the side lengths of a triangle work in the Pythagorean equation, must the triangle be a right triangle? You'll explore this question in the investigation.

## Investigation: Is the Converse True?

For this investigation you will need string, three paper clips, and two helpers. If no one is available to help you, you will need string, some pins or tacks, and a large sheet of thick cardboard.

A set of three positive integers that satisfy the Pythagorean formula is called a **Pythagorean triple.** For example, the integers 3, 4, and 5 are a Pythagorean triple because $3^2 + 4^2 = 5^2$.

Page 484 of your book lists nine examples of Pythagorean triples. Select one triple from the list, and mark off four points—*A*, *B*, *C*, and *D*—on a string to create three consecutive lengths from your set of triples. (Leave some string to the left of *A* and to the right of *D* so that you will be able to tie a knot.) For example, if you choose 5, 12, 13, you could mark your string like this:

$$A \quad B \qquad\quad C \qquad\qquad D$$
$$|\ 5\ \text{in.}\ |\!\leftarrow\!\!-12\ \text{in.}\!\rightarrow\!|\!\leftarrow\!\!-13\ \text{in.}\!\rightarrow\!|$$

Tie the ends of the string together so that points *A* and *D* meet.

If you are working with two other people:

- Loop three paper clips onto the string.
- Three people should each pull a paper clip at point *A*, *B*, or *C* to stretch the string tight and form a triangle. (See the photograph in your book.)
- Measure the largest angle of the triangle. What type of triangle is formed?

If you are working by yourself:

- Pin the string to the cardboard at one of the marked points.
- Stretch the part of the string between the pinned-down point and the next marked point tight. Pin that point down. Then pull on the third marked point to stretch the string tight and form a triangle, and pin down that point.

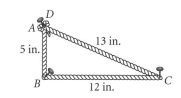

- Measure the largest angle of the triangle. What type of triangle is formed?

*(continued)*

Select at least one more triple from the list and repeat the experiment.

Your results can be summarized as a conjecture.

> **Converse of the Pythagorean Theorem**  If the lengths of the three sides of a triangle satisfy the Pythagorean equation, then the triangle is a right triangle.  **C-82**

On page 486 of your book, read the beginning of a proof of the Converse of the Pythagorean Theorem. Then complete the proof using the model below.

$\triangle DEF$ is a right triangle. So, by the Pythagorean Theorem, $a^2 + b^2 = x^2$.

But we were given that $a^2 + b^2 = c^2$.

Therefore, by substitution, $x^2 = $ _____.

Take the square root of each side to get _____ = _____.

We now know that $\triangle ABC \cong \triangle DEF$ by _____, so $\angle C \cong \angle F$ by _____.
Thus, $m\angle C = m\angle F = 90°$, so $\triangle ABC$ is a right triangle.

**EXAMPLE**  Les wanted to build a rectangular pen for his guinea pig. When he finished, he measured the bottom of the pen. He found that one side was 54 inches long, the adjacent side was 30 inches long, and one diagonal was 63 inches long. Is the pen really rectangular?

▶ **Solution**  If the pen is rectangular, then two adjacent sides and a diagonal will form a right triangle. To see if this is the case, check whether the measurements form a Pythagorean triple.

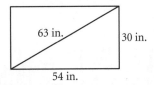

$30^2 + 54^2 = 900 + 2916 = 3816$ and $63^2 = 3969$

Because $30^2 + 54^2 \neq 63^2$, the measurements are not a Pythagorean triple, so the triangle is not a right triangle. Therefore, the pen is not rectangular.

# Two Special Right Triangles

In this lesson you will

- Discover a shortcut for finding an unknown side length in an **isosceles right triangle** (also called a **45°-45°-90° triangle**)
- Discover a shortcut for finding an unknown side length in a **30°-60°-90° triangle**

An isosceles right triangle is sometimes called a 45°-45°-90° triangle because of its angle measures. Note that an isosceles right triangle is half of a square.

In the next investigation you will discover the relationship among the side lengths of an isosceles right triangle.

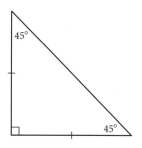

## Investigation 1: Isosceles Right Triangles

The isosceles right triangle at right has legs of length $l$ and a hypotenuse of length $h$. If you know the value of $l$, you can use the Pythagorean Theorem to find $h$. Here are two examples.

- If $l$ is 5, then $h^2 = 5^2 + 5^2 = 50$, so $h = \sqrt{50} = \sqrt{25 \cdot 2} = 5\sqrt{2}$.
- If $l$ is 8, then $h^2 = 8^2 + 8^2 = 128$, so $h = \sqrt{128} = \sqrt{64 \cdot 2} = 8\sqrt{2}$.

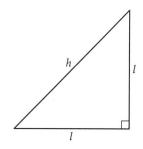

Find the value of $h$ for at least three more integer values of $l$. Simplify the square root, but leave it in radical form.

Look for a pattern in the relationship between $l$ and $h$. Summarize your findings by completing this conjecture.

**Isosceles Right Triangle Conjecture** In an isosceles right triangle, if the legs have length $l$, then the hypotenuse has length _____.

**C-83**

If you fold an equilateral triangle along one of its lines of symmetry, you get a 30°-60°-90° triangle, as shown at right. Triangle $ABC$ is equilateral and $\overline{CD}$ is an angle bisector.

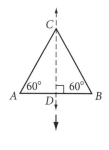

Prove that $\triangle ACD \cong \triangle BCD$ and then answer the questions posed on page 492 of your book. You can check your answers with the sample answers below.

1. Why must the angles in $\triangle BCD$ be 30°, 60°, and 90°?

   $m\angle B = 60°$ because $\triangle ABC$ is equilateral and therefore equiangular. By the same reasoning, $m\angle ACB = 60°$. Angle bisector $\overline{CD}$ cuts $\angle ACB$ into two congruent angles, so $m\angle ACD = 30°$ and $m\angle BCD = 30°$. Using the Triangle Sum Conjecture, $m\angle CDB = 90°$.

2. How does $BD$ compare to $AB$? How does $BD$ compare to $BC$?

   By the Vertex Angle Bisector Conjecture, $\overline{CD}$ is a median to $\overline{AB}$, so $AD = BD$ and $BD = \frac{1}{2}AB$. Because $\triangle ABC$ is equilateral, $AB = BC$, so $BD = \frac{1}{2}BC$.

3. In any 30°-60°-90° triangle, how does the length of the hypotenuse compare to the length of the shorter leg?

   The length of the hypotenuse is twice the length of the shorter leg.

**(continued)**

## Investigation 2: 30°-60°-90° Triangles

Below is a 30°-60°-90° triangle. If you know the length of the shorter leg, $a$, you can find the length of the other sides. For example, if $a$ is 3, then the hypotenuse, $c$, is 6. Use the Pythagorean formula to find the length of the other leg, $b$.

$$3^2 + b^2 = 6^2$$

$$9 + b^2 = 36$$

$$b^2 = 27$$

$$b = \sqrt{27} = \sqrt{9 \cdot 3} = 3\sqrt{3}$$

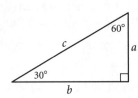

The length of leg $b$ is $3\sqrt{3}$ units.

Copy the table from Step 2 of Investigation 2, and repeat the procedure above to complete the table. Write the length of the longer leg in simplified radical form. Look for a pattern between the lengths of the legs of each triangle. Use your observations to complete the conjecture.

---

**30°-60°-90° Triangle Conjecture** In a 30°-60°-90° triangle, if the shorter leg has length $a$, then the longer leg has length _____ and the hypotenuse has length $2a$.

**C-84**

---

Page 493 of your book gives a proof of the 30°-60°-90° Triangle Conjecture. Read the proof and make sure you understand it. Then read the example below.

**EXAMPLE** | Find the lettered side lengths. All lengths are in centimeters.

a.
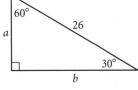

b.
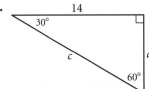

▸ **Solution** | a. The length of the shorter leg is half the length of the hypotenuse, so $a = 13$ cm. The length of the longer leg is the length of the shorter leg times $\sqrt{3}$, so $b = 13\sqrt{3}$ cm, or about 22.5 cm.

b. The length of the longer leg is the length of the shorter leg times $\sqrt{3}$, so $14 = a\sqrt{3}$ and $a = \frac{14}{\sqrt{3}}$ cm, or about 8.1 cm. The length of the hypotenuse is twice the length of the shorter leg, so $c = \frac{28}{\sqrt{3}}$ cm, or about 16.2 cm.

# 9.4 Story Problems

In this lesson you will

- Use the Pythagorean Theorem to **solve problems**

You can use the Pythagorean Theorem to solve many problems involving right triangles.

Read the example in your text. Notice that the problem in that example requires applying the Pythagorean Theorem twice, first to find the diagonal of the bottom of the box and then to find the diagonal of the box.

In the examples below, try to solve each problem on your own before reading the solution.

**EXAMPLE A** | A square has a diagonal of length 16 inches. What is the area of the square?

▶ **Solution** | The diagonal of a square divides the square into two 45°-45°-90° triangles. To find the area of the square, you need to know the leg length, $l$, of the triangles.

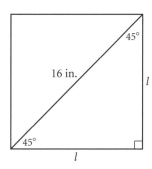

By the Isosceles Right Triangle Conjecture (or by the Pythagorean Theorem), you know that $l \cdot \sqrt{2} = 16$, so $l = \frac{16}{\sqrt{2}}$ in. Therefore,

$$\text{Area of square} = \frac{16}{\sqrt{2}} \cdot \frac{16}{\sqrt{2}}$$

$$= \frac{256}{2}$$

$$= 128$$

So, the area of the square is 128 in².

(continued)

**EXAMPLE B** | The Clementina High School Marching Band is practicing on the school football field. The field is 300 feet long from west to east and 160 feet wide from north to south. Len starts at the southwest corner and marches at a rate of 5 feet per second toward the southeast corner. At the same time, Jen begins marching diagonally from the northwest corner toward the southeast corner. If they want to meet at the corner at the same instant, how fast does Jen need to march?

▶ **Solution** | To start, make a sketch to illustrate the problem.

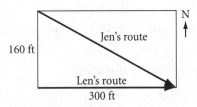

Len marches 300 feet at a rate of 5 feet per second, so it will take him $300 \div 5$, or 60 seconds, to reach the southeast corner.

For them to meet at the same time, Jen must also cover her route in 60 seconds. To find the distance Jen must march, use the Pythagorean Theorem.

$$160^2 + 300^2 = x^2$$

$$25{,}600 + 90{,}000 = x^2$$

$$115{,}600 = x^2$$

$$340 = x$$

Jen must cover 340 feet in 60 seconds, so she must march at a rate of $340 \div 60$, or about 5.7 feet per second.

# 9.5  Distance in Coordinate Geometry

In this lesson you will

- Learn a formula for finding the **distance between two points** on a coordinate plane
- Discover the **general equation of a circle**

On a coordinate plane, you can find the length of a segment in the *x*-direction by counting grid squares or by subtracting *x*-coordinates. Similarly, you can find the length of a segment in the *y*-direction by counting or by subtracting *y*-coordinates.

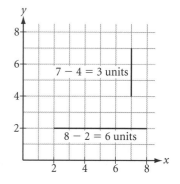

You can think of any segment that is not in the *x*- or *y*-direction as the hypotenuse of a right triangle with legs in the *x*- and *y*-directions. This allows you to use the Pythagorean Theorem to find the length of the segment.

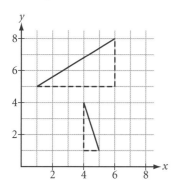

In the next investigation you'll use this idea to develop a formula for the distance between any two points on a coordinate plane.

## Investigation: The Distance Formula

Step 1 in your book shows four segments on coordinate planes. Find the length of each segment by considering it to be the hypotenuse of a right triangle. For example, the segment in part a is the hypotenuse of a right triangle with legs of lengths 2 units and 4 units, so, using the Pythagorean Theorem,

$$\text{length}^2 = 2^2 + 4^2$$

$$= 20$$

$$\text{length} = \sqrt{20} = 2\sqrt{5} \approx 4.5 \text{ units}$$

In Step 2, you must plot and connect the points and then find the distance between them. You can find the distance using the procedure you used in Step 1.

Consider the points $A(15, 34)$ and $B(42, 70)$. It wouldn't be practical to plot these points on a grid, so how can you find the distance between them?

(continued)

Recall that you can find a horizontal distance by subtracting $x$-coordinates and a vertical distance by subtracting $y$-coordinates. Use this idea to complete Steps 3–5 in your book and find the distance between points $A(15, 34)$ and $B(42, 70)$.

You can generalize your findings from this investigation as a conjecture.

> **Distance Formula** The distance between points $A(x_1, y_1)$ and $B(x_2, y_2)$ is given by the formula $(AB)^2 = (x_2 - x_1)^2 + (y_2 - y_1)^2$ or $AB = \sqrt{(x_2 - x_1)^2 + (y_2 - y_1)^2}$.   **C-85**

Example A in your book shows how to apply the distance formula. Read Example A.

Example B shows how to use the distance formula to write the equation of a circle with center $(5, 4)$ and radius 7 units. The solution uses the fact that the circle is the set of all points $(x, y)$ that are 7 units from the fixed point $(5, 4)$. Read Example B and then read the example below.

**EXAMPLE** | Write the equation for the circle at right.

▶ **Solution** | The circle has center $(0, -3)$ and radius 3 units. Let $(x, y)$ represent any point on the circle. The distance from $(x, y)$ to the circle's center, $(0, -3)$, is 3. Substitute this information in the distance formula.

$(x - 0)^2 + (y - (-3))^2 = 3^2$, or $x^2 + (y + 3)^2 = 3^2$

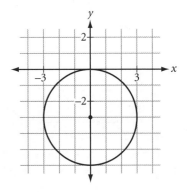

In the Mini-Investigation in Exercise 11, you'll develop the general equation of a circle.

# Circles and the Pythagorean Theorem

In this lesson you will

- Use **circle conjectures** and the **Pythagorean Theorem** to solve problems

In Chapter 6, you discovered a number of properties of circles that involved right angles. Here are two of the conjectures from that chapter.

**Tangent Conjecture:** A tangent to a circle is perpendicular to the radius drawn to the point of tangency.

**Angles Inscribed in a Semicircle Conjecture:** Angles inscribed in a semicircle are right angles.

You can use these and other circle conjectures and the Pythagorean Theorem to solve some challenging problems.

Examples A and B in your book use circle conjectures, dissections, special right triangle relationships, and the Pythagorean Theorem. Read these examples and follow each step in the solutions. Below are two more examples.

**EXAMPLE A** | $\overrightarrow{AP}$ and $\overrightarrow{AQ}$ are tangent to circle $O$, and $AP = 3$ cm. Find the area of the shaded region.

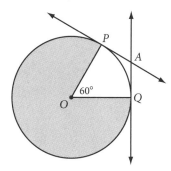

▶ **Solution** | You can draw $\overline{OA}$ to create two 30°-60°-90° triangles. (How do you know the segment bisects $\angle O$ to create two 30° angles?)

In $\triangle APO$, the shorter leg, $\overline{AP}$, has length 3 cm, so the longer leg, which is the radius of the circle, has length $3\sqrt{3}$ cm.

Because the radius is $3\sqrt{3}$ cm, the area of the entire circle is $27\pi$ cm². The area of the shaded region is $\frac{360 - 60}{360}$, or $\frac{5}{6}$, of the area of the circle. So, the shaded area is $\frac{5}{6}(27\pi) = \frac{45}{2}\pi$ cm², or about 70.7 cm².

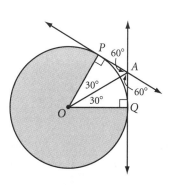

(continued)

**EXAMPLE B** | Find the area of the shaded region.

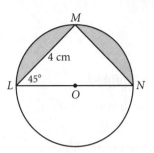

▶ **Solution** | The area of the shaded region is the area of the semicircle minus the area of △LMN.

Because ∠LMN is inscribed in a semicircle, it is a right angle. Using the Triangle Sum Conjecture, $m\angle N = 45°$. Therefore, △LMN is an isosceles right triangle (a 45°-45°-90° triangle) with a leg of length 4 cm.

The length of the hypotenuse, which is the diameter of the circle, is $4\sqrt{2}$ cm. The radius of the circle is then $2\sqrt{2}$ cm, so the area of the entire circle is $\pi\left(2\sqrt{2}\right)^2$, or $8\pi$ cm². Therefore, the area of the semicircle is $4\pi$ cm². The area of △LMN is $\frac{1}{2} \cdot 4 \cdot 4$, or 8 cm². So, the area of the shaded region is $(4\pi - 8)$ cm², or about 4.6 cm².

# 10.1 The Geometry of Solids

In this lesson you will

- Learn about **polyhedrons,** including **prisms** and **pyramids**
- Learn about solids with curved surfaces, including **cylinders, cones,** and **spheres**

In this chapter you will study three-dimensional solid figures. Lesson 10.1 introduces various types of three-dimensional solids and the terminology associated with them. Read the lesson. Then review what you read by completing the statements and answering the questions below.

**1.** A polyhedron is a solid formed by _____ that enclose a single region of space.

**2.** A segment where two faces of a polyhedron intersect is called a(n) _____.

**3.** A polyhedron with six faces is called a(n) _____.

**4.** A tetrahedron has _____ faces.

**5.** If each face of a polyhedron is enclosed by a regular polygon, and each face is congruent to the other faces, and the faces meet each vertex in exactly the same way, then the polyhedron is called a(n) _____.

**6.** A(n) _____ is a polyhedron with two faces, called bases, that are congruent, parallel polygons.

**7.** The faces of a prism that are not bases are called _____.

**8.** What is the difference between a right prism and an oblique prism?

**9.** What type of solid is shown below?

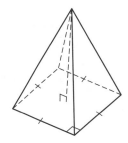

**10.** How many bases does a pyramid have?

**11.** The point that all the lateral faces of a pyramid have in common is the _____ of the pyramid.

**12.** What is the difference between an altitude of a pyramid and the height of a pyramid?

**13.** What type of solid is shown at right?

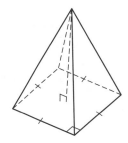

(continued)

**14.** Name three types of solids with curved surfaces.

**15.** A(n) _____ is the set of all points in space at a given distance from a given point.

**16.** A circle that encloses the base of a hemisphere is called a(n) _____.

**17.** Give an example of a real object that is shaped like a cylinder. Explain how you know it is a cylinder.

**18.** Tell which cylinder below is an oblique cylinder and which is a right cylinder. For each cylinder, draw and label the *axis* and the *altitude*.

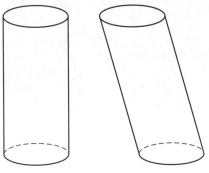

**19.** The base of a cone is a(n) _____.

**20.** If the line segment connecting the vertex of a cone with the center of the base is perpendicular to the base, then the cone is a(n) _____.

After you have finished, check your answers below.

**1.** polygons

**2.** edge

**3.** hexahedron

**4.** four

**5.** regular polygon

**6.** prism

**7.** lateral faces

**8.** In a right prism all lateral faces are rectangles and are perpendicular to the base. In an oblique prism they are not.

**9.** pentagonal prism (it may be oblique or right)

**10.** one

**11.** vertex

**12.** The altitude is a segment from the vertex of the pyramid to the plane of the base that is perpendicular to the plane of the base. The height is the length of the altitude.

**13.** square pyramid

**14.** possible answers: cylinder, cone, sphere, hemisphere

**15.** sphere

**16.** great circle

**17.** The example will vary. Reason: It has two parallel bases and both bases are circles.

**18.** The figure on the left is a right cylinder, and the figure on the right is an oblique cylinder. See page 523 of the book for labeled pictures of both.

**19.** circle

**20.** right cone

# 10.2 Volume of Prisms and Cylinders

In this lesson you will

- Discover the volume formula for **right rectangular prisms**
- Extend the volume formula to **right prisms** and **right cylinders**
- Extend the volume formula to **oblique prisms** and **oblique cylinders**

**Volume** is the measure of the amount of space contained in a solid. You use cubic units to measure volume: cubic inches $(in^3)$, cubic feet $(ft^3)$, cubic yards $(yd^3)$, cubic centimeters $(cm^3)$, cubic meters $(m^3)$, and so on. The volume of an object is the number of unit cubes that completely fill the space within the object.

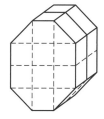

Length: 1 unit     Volume: 1 cubic unit     Volume: 20 cubic units

## Investigation: The Volume Formula for Prisms and Cylinders

Read Step 1 of the investigation in your book.

Notice that the number of cubes in the base layer is the number of square units in the area of the base and that the number of layers is the height of the prism. So, you can use the area of the base and the height to find the volume of a right rectangular prism.

> **Rectangular Prism Volume Conjecture** If $B$ is the area of the base of a right rectangular prism and $H$ is the height of the solid, then the formula for the volume is $V = $ _____ .
>
> **C-86a**

You can find the volume of any other right prism or cylinder the same way—by multiplying the area of the base by the height. For example, to find the volume of this cylinder, find the area of the circular base (the number of cubes in the base layer) and multiply by the height.

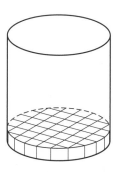

You can extend the Rectangular Prism Volume Conjecture to all right prisms and right cylinders. Complete the conjecture below.

> **Right Prism-Cylinder Volume Conjecture** If $B$ is the area of the base of a right prism (or cylinder) and $H$ is the height of the solid, then the formula for the volume is $V = $ _____ .
>
> **C-86b**

(continued)

What about the volume of an *oblique* prism or cylinder? Page 532 of your book shows that you can model an oblique rectangular prism with a slanted stack of paper. You can then "straighten" the stack to form a right rectangular prism with the same volume. The right prism has the same base area and the same height as the oblique prism. So, you find the volume of the oblique prism by multiplying the area of its base by its height. A similar argument works for other oblique prisms and cylinders.

Now you can extend the Right Prism-Cylinder Volume Conjecture to oblique prisms and cylinders.

> **Oblique Prism-Cylinder Volume Conjecture** The volume of an oblique prism (or cylinder) is the same as the volume of a right prism (or cylinder) that has the same _____ and the same _____.          **C-86c**

Be careful when calculating the volume of an oblique prism or cylinder. Because the lateral edges are not perpendicular to the bases, the height of the prism or cylinder is *not* the length of a lateral edge.

You can combine the last three conjectures into one conjecture.

> **Prism-Cylinder Volume Conjecture** The volume of a prism or a cylinder is the _____ multiplied by the _____.          **C-86**

Examples A and B in your book show you how to find the volumes of a trapezoidal prism and an oblique cylinder. Read both examples. Try to find the volumes yourself before reading the solutions. Then read the example below.

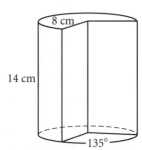

**EXAMPLE** | The solid at right is a right cylinder with a 135° slice removed. Find the volume of the solid. Round your answer to the nearest cm.

► **Solution** | The base is $\frac{225}{360}$, or $\frac{5}{8}$, of a circle with radius 8 cm. The whole circle has area $64\pi$ cm², so the base has area $\frac{5}{8}(64\pi)$, or $40\pi$ cm². Now use the volume formula.

$V = BH$          The volume formula.

$\quad = 40\pi(14)$          Substitute the area of the base and the height.

$\quad = 560\pi$          Multiply.

$\quad \approx 1759$          Use the $\pi$ key on your calculator to get an approximate answer.

The volume is about 1759 cm³.

# CONDENSED
# LESSON
# 10.3 Volume of Pyramids and Cones

In this lesson you will

- Discover the volume formula for **pyramids** and **cones**

There is a simple relationship between the volumes of prisms and pyramids with congruent bases and the same height, and between cylinders and cones with congruent bases and the same height.

## Investigation: The Volume Formula for Pyramids and Cones

If you have the materials listed at the beginning of the investigation, follow the steps in your book before continuing. The text below summarizes the results of the investigation.

Suppose you start with a prism and a pyramid with congruent bases and the same height. If you fill the pyramid with sand or water and then pour the contents into the prism three times, you will exactly fill the prism. In other words, the volume of the pyramid is $\frac{1}{3}$ the volume of the prism.

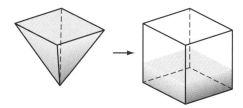

You will get the same result no matter what shape the bases have, as long as the base of the pyramid is congruent to the base of the prism and the heights are the same.

If you repeat the experiment with a cone and a cylinder with congruent bases and the same height, you will get the same result. That is, you can empty the contents of the cone into the cylinder exactly three times.

The results can be summarized in a conjecture.

---

**Pyramid-Cone Volume Conjecture** If $B$ is the area of the base of a pyramid or a cone and $H$ is the height of the solid, then the formula for the volume is $V = \frac{1}{3}BH$.

`C-87`

---

Example A in your book shows how to find the volume of a regular hexagonal pyramid. In the example, you need to use the 30°-60°-90° Triangle Conjecture to find the apothem of the base. Example B involves the volume of a cone. Work through both examples. Then read the example on the next page.

(continued)

**EXAMPLE** | Find the volume of this triangular pyramid.

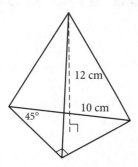

▶ **Solution** | The base is an isosceles right triangle. To find the area of the base, you need to know the lengths of the legs. Let $l$ be the length of a leg, and use the Isosceles Right Triangle Conjecture.

$l(\sqrt{2}) = 10$ — The length of the hypotenuse is the length of a leg times $\sqrt{2}$.

$l = \dfrac{10}{\sqrt{2}}$ — Solve for $l$.

The length of each leg is $\dfrac{10}{\sqrt{2}}$. Now find the area of the triangle.

$A = \dfrac{1}{2}bh$ — Area formula for triangles.

$= \dfrac{1}{2}\left(\dfrac{10}{\sqrt{2}}\right)\left(\dfrac{10}{\sqrt{2}}\right)$ — Substitute the known values.

$= 25$ — Multiply.

So, the base has area 25 cm$^2$. Now find the volume of the pyramid.

$V = \dfrac{1}{3}BH$ — Volume formula for pyramids and cones.

$= \dfrac{1}{3}(25)(12)$ — Substitute the known values.

$= 100$ — Multiply.

The volume of the pyramid is 100 cm$^3$.

# Volume Problems

**CONDENSED**
**LESSON**
**10.4**

In this lesson you will

- Use the volume formulas you have learned to **solve problems**

You have learned volume formulas for prisms, cylinders, pyramids, and cones. In this lesson you will use these formulas to solve problems.

In Example A in your book, the volume of a right triangular prism is given and you must find the height. In Example B, the volume of a sector of a right cylinder is given and you must find the radius of the base. Try to solve the problems yourself before reading the solutions. Below are some more examples.

**EXAMPLE A** | A swimming pool is in the shape of the prism shown at right. How many gallons of water can the pool hold? (A cubic foot of water is about 7.5 gallons.)

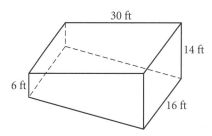

▶ **Solution** | First, find the volume of the pool in cubic feet. The pool is in the shape of a trapezoidal prism. The trapezoid has bases of length 6 feet and 14 feet and a height of 30 feet. The height of the prism is 16 feet.

$$V = BH \qquad \text{Volume formula for prisms.}$$

$$= \frac{1}{2}(30)(6 + 14) \cdot 16 \qquad \text{Use the formula } \frac{1}{2}h(b_1 + b_2) \text{ for the area of a trapezoid.}$$

$$= 4800 \qquad \text{Solve.}$$

The pool has volume 4800 ft³. A cubic foot is about 7.5 gallons, so the pool holds 4800(7.5), or 36,000 gallons of water.

**EXAMPLE B** | A sealed rectangular container 5 cm by 14 cm by 20 cm is sitting on its smallest face. It is filled with water up to 5 cm from the top. How many centimeters from the bottom will the water level reach if the container is placed on its largest face?

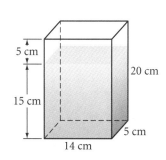

▶ **Solution** | The smallest face is a 5-by-14-centimeter rectangle. When the prism is resting on its smallest face, the water is in the shape of a rectangular prism with base area 70 cm² and height 15 cm. So, the volume of the water is 1050 cm³.

(continued)

If the container is placed on its largest face, the volume will still be 1050 cm³, but the base area and height will change. The area of the new base will be 14(20), or 280 cm². You can use the volume formula to find the height.

$V = BH$      Volume formula for prisms.

$1050 = 280H$      Substitute the known values.

$3.75 = H$      Solve for $H$.

The height of the water will be 3.75 cm. So, the water level will be 3.75 cm from the bottom of the container.

**EXAMPLE C**

Find the volume of a rectangular prism with dimensions that are twice those of another rectangular prism with volume 120 cm³.

▶ **Solution**

For the rectangular prism with volume 120 cm³, let the dimensions of the rectangular base be $x$ and $y$ and the height be $z$. The volume of this prism is $xyz$, so $xyz = 120$.

The dimensions of the base of the other prism are $2x$ and $2y$, and the height is $2z$. Let $V$ be the volume of this prism. Then

$V = BH$      Volume formula for prisms.

$= (2x)(2y)(2z)$      Substitute the known values.

$= 8xyz$      Multiply.

$= 8(120)$      Substitute the known value.

$= 960$      Multiply.

The volume of the larger prism is 960 cm³.

# CONDENSED LESSON

# 10.5 Displacement and Density

In this lesson you will

- Learn how the idea of **displacement** can be used to find the volume of an object
- Learn how to calculate the **density** of an object

To find the volumes of geometric solids, such as prisms and cones, you can use a volume formula. But what if you want to find the volume of an irregularly shaped object like a rock? As Example A in your book illustrates, you can submerge the object in a regularly shaped container filled with water. The volume of water that is **displaced** will be the same as the volume of the object. Read Example A in your book. Then read the example below.

**EXAMPLE A** | When Tom puts a rock into a cylindrical container with diameter 7 cm, the water level rises 3 cm. What is the volume of the rock to the nearest tenth of a cubic centimeter?

▶ **Solution** | The "slice" of water that is displaced is a cylinder with diameter 7 cm and height 3 cm.

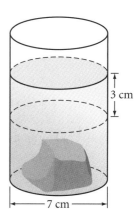

Use the volume formula to find the volume of the displaced water.

$V = BH$

$\quad = \pi(3.5)^2 \cdot 3$

$\quad \approx 115.5$

The volume of the rock is about 115.5 cm³, the same as the volume of the displaced water.

An important property of a material is its density. **Density** is the mass of matter in a given volume. It is calculated by dividing mass by volume.

$$\text{density} = \frac{\text{mass}}{\text{volume}}$$

The table on page 551 of your book gives the densities of ten metals. In Example B, the mass of a clump of metal and information about the amount of water it displaces are used to identify the type of metal. Read this example carefully. Then read the following example.

(continued)

**EXAMPLE B**   Chemist Preethi Bhatt is given a clump of metal and is told that it is sodium. She finds that the metal has a mass of 184.3 g. She places it into a nonreactive liquid in a cylindrical beaker with base diameter 10 cm. If the metal is indeed sodium, how high should the liquid level rise?

▶ **Solution**   The table on page 551 of your book indicates that the density of sodium is 0.97 g/cm³. Use the density formula to find what the volume of the clump of metal should be if it is sodium.

$$\text{density} = \frac{\text{mass}}{\text{volume}} \qquad \text{Density formula.}$$

$$0.97 = \frac{184.3}{\text{volume}} \qquad \text{Substitute the known information.}$$

$$\text{volume} \cdot 0.97 = 184.3 \qquad \text{Multiply both sides by } volume.$$

$$\text{volume} = \frac{184.3}{0.97} \qquad \text{Divide both sides by 0.97.}$$

$$\text{volume} = 190 \qquad \text{Simplify.}$$

So, if the metal is sodium, it should displace 190 cm³ of water. Use the volume formula to find the height of the liquid that should be displaced.

$$V = BH \qquad \text{Volume formula for cylinders.}$$

$$190 = (5^2\pi)H \qquad \text{Substitute the known information. (The base is a circle with radius 5 cm.)}$$

$$190 = 25\pi H \qquad \text{Multiply.}$$

$$2.4 \approx H \qquad \text{Solve for } H.$$

The liquid should rise about 2.4 cm.

# Volume of a Sphere

In this lesson you will

- Discover the volume formula for a **sphere**

You can find the volume of a sphere by comparing it to the volume of a cylinder. In the investigation you will see how.

## Investigation: The Formula for the Volume of a Sphere

If you have the materials listed at the beginning of the investigation, follow the steps in your book before continuing. The text below summarizes the results of the investigation.

Suppose you have a hemisphere and a cylinder. The radius of the cylinder equals the radius of the hemisphere, and the height of the cylinder is twice the radius. Note that the cylinder is the smallest one that would enclose a sphere made from two of the hemispheres.

The volume of the cylinder is $\pi r^2 (2r)$, or $2\pi r^3$.

If you fill the hemisphere with sand or water and empty the contents into the cylinder, the cylinder will be $\frac{1}{3}$ full.

If you fill the hemisphere again and empty the contents into the cylinder, the cylinder will be $\frac{2}{3}$ full. So, the volume of the sphere (two hemispheres) is equal to $\frac{2}{3}$ the volume of the cylinder.

The volume of the cylinder is $2\pi r^3$. So, the volume of the sphere is $\frac{2}{3}(2\pi r^3)$, or $\frac{4}{3}\pi r^3$.

The results can be summarized as a conjecture.

**Sphere Volume Conjecture** The volume of a sphere with radius $r$ is given by the formula $V = \frac{4}{3}\pi r^3$.   **C-88**

Read Example A in your book, which involves finding the percentage of plaster cut away when the largest possible sphere is carved from a cube. The solution involves four steps:

**Step 1**  Find the volume of the sphere.

**Step 2**  Find the volume of the cube.

**Step 3**  Subtract the volume of the sphere from the volume of the cube to find the volume of the plaster cut away.

**Step 4**  Divide the volume cut away by the volume of the original cube and convert the answer to a percent to find the percentage cut away.

Read Example B in your book. Solve the problem yourself and then check your work by reading the given solution.

The following two examples give you more practice working with the volume of a sphere.

(continued)

**EXAMPLE A**

Find the volume of this solid.

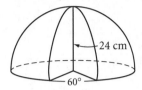

24 cm

60°

▶ **Solution**

The solid is a hemisphere with a 60° sector cut away. First, find the volume of the entire hemisphere. Because the formula for the volume of a sphere is $V = \frac{4}{3}\pi r^3$, the formula for the volume of a hemisphere is $V = \frac{2}{3}\pi r^3$.

$$V = \frac{2}{3}\pi r^3 \qquad \text{Volume formula for a hemisphere.}$$

$$= \frac{2}{3}\pi(24)^3 \qquad \text{The radius is 24 cm.}$$

$$= 9216\pi \qquad \text{Simplify.}$$

The volume of the entire hemisphere is $9216\pi$ cm³. A 60° sector has been cut away, so the fraction of the hemisphere that remains is $\frac{300}{360}$, or $\frac{5}{6}$. So, the volume of the solid is $\frac{5}{6}(9216\pi) = 7680\pi$ cm³, or about 24,127 cm³.

**EXAMPLE B**

A marble is submerged in water in a rectangular prism with a 2 cm-by-2 cm base. The water in the prism rises 0.9 cm when the marble is submerged. What is the diameter of the marble?

▶ **Solution**

First find the volume of the water displaced by the marble.

$$V = BH \qquad \text{Volume formula for a prism.}$$

$$= (2)(2)(0.9) \qquad \text{Substitute the known information.}$$

$$= 3.6 \qquad \text{Simplify.}$$

So, the volume of the displaced water, and thus of the marble, is 3.6 cm³.

Next use the volume of the marble to find its radius. Substitute 3.6 for $V$ in the formula for the volume of a sphere and solve for $r$.

$$V = \frac{4}{3}\pi r^3 \qquad \text{Volume formula for a sphere.}$$

$$3.6 = \frac{4}{3}\pi r^3 \qquad \text{Substitute the known information.}$$

$$\frac{\frac{3}{4}(3.6)}{\pi} = r^3 \qquad \text{Multiply both sides by } \tfrac{3}{4} \text{ and divide by } \pi.$$

$$0.86 \approx r^3 \qquad \text{Simplify.}$$

$$r \approx \sqrt[3]{0.86} \approx 0.95 \qquad \text{Take the cube root of both sides.}$$

The radius of the marble is about 0.95 cm, so the diameter is about 1.9 cm.

*Discovering Geometry Condensed Lessons*
©2008 Key Curriculum Press

# 10.7 Surface Area of a Sphere

In this lesson you will

- Discover the formula for the **surface area of a sphere**

You can use the formula for the volume of a sphere, $V = \frac{4}{3}\pi r^3$, to find the formula for the surface area of a sphere.

## Investigation: The Formula for the Surface Area of a Sphere

Imagine a sphere's surface divided into tiny shapes that are nearly flat. The surface area of the sphere is equal to the sum of the areas of these "near polygons." If you imagine radii connecting each of the vertices of the "near polygons" to the center of the sphere, you are mentally dividing the volume of the sphere into many "near pyramids." Each of the "near polygons" is a base for one of the pyramids, and the radius, $r$, of the sphere is the height of the pyramid. The volume, $V$, of the sphere is the sum of the volumes of all the pyramids.

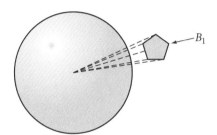

**Step 1** Imagine that the surface of a sphere is divided into 1000 "near polygons" with areas $B_1, B_2, B_3, \ldots, B_{1000}$. The surface area, $S$, of the sphere is the sum of the areas of these "near polygons":

$$S = B_1 + B_2 + B_3 + \cdots + B_{1000}$$

**Step 2** The pyramid with base area $B_1$ has volume $\frac{1}{3}(B_1)r$, the pyramid with base area $B_2$ has volume $\frac{1}{3}(B_2)r$, and so on. The volume of the sphere, $V$, is the sum of these volumes:

$$V = \frac{1}{3}(B_1)r + \frac{1}{3}(B_2)r + \frac{1}{3}(B_3)r + \cdots + \frac{1}{3}(B_{1000})r$$

Factor $\frac{1}{3}r$ from each term on the right side of the equation:

$$V = \frac{1}{3}r(B_1 + B_2 + B_3 + \cdots + B_{1000})$$

**Step 3** Because $V = \frac{4}{3}\pi r^3$, you can substitute $\frac{4}{3}\pi r^3$ for $V$:

$$\frac{4}{3}\pi r^3 = \frac{1}{3}r(B_1 + B_2 + B_3 + \cdots + B_{1000})$$

Now substitute $S$ for $B_1 + B_2 + B_3 + \cdots + B_{1000}$:

$$\frac{4}{3}\pi r^3 = \frac{1}{3}rS$$

(continued)

**Step 4**   Solve the last equation for the surface area, $S$.

$\frac{4}{3}\pi r^3 = \frac{1}{3}rS$     The equation from Step 3.

$4\pi r^3 = rS$      Multiply both sides by 3.

$4\pi r^2 = S$      Divide both sides by $r$.

You now have a formula for finding the surface area of a sphere in terms of the radius. You can state the result as a conjecture.

> **Sphere Surface Area Conjecture**   The surface area, $S$, of a sphere with radius $r$ is given by the formula $S = 4\pi r^2$.     `C-89`

The example in your book shows how to find the surface area of a sphere if you know its volume. Try to find the surface area on your own before reading the solution. Then solve the problem in the example below.

**EXAMPLE** | The base of this hemisphere has circumference $32\pi$ cm. Find the surface area of the hemisphere (including the base).

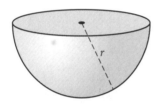

▶ **Solution** | Because the base of the hemisphere has circumference $32\pi$ cm, the radius is 16 cm.

The area of the base of the hemisphere is $\pi(16)^2$, or $256\pi$ cm$^2$.

The area of the curved surface is half the surface area of a sphere with radius 16 cm.

$S = \frac{1}{2} \cdot 4\pi r^2$

$= \frac{1}{2} \cdot 4\pi(16)^2$

$= 512\pi$

So, the total surface area is $256\pi + 512\pi = 768\pi$ cm$^2$, or about 2413 cm$^2$.

# 11.1 Similar Polygons

In this lesson you will

- Learn what it means for two figures to be **similar**
- Use the definition of similarity to **find missing measures** in similar polygons
- Explore **dilations** of figures on a coordinate plane

You know that figures that have the same size and shape are *congruent figures.* Figures that have the same shape but not necessarily the same size are **similar figures.** You can think of similar figures as enlargements or reductions of one another with no distortion. The pentagons below are similar. The rectangles are *not* similar. You could not enlarge or reduce one rectangle to fit exactly over the other.

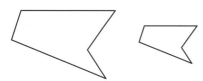

These pentagons are similar.          These rectangles are *not* similar.

In the investigation you will explore what makes polygons similar.

## Investigation 1: What Makes Polygons Similar?

Hexagons *ABCDEF* and *PQRSTU* in your book are similar. Use patty paper to compare the corresponding angles. You should find that the corresponding angles are congruent.

Now carefully measure the corresponding sides and find the ratio of each side length of *ABCDEF* to the corresponding side length of *PQRSTU*. You should find that each ratio is approximately equal to $\frac{5}{9}$. So, the corresponding sides are proportional.

Finally, calculate and compare these side length ratios within each polygon: $\frac{AB}{BC}$ with $\frac{PQ}{QR}$ and $\frac{EF}{CD}$ with $\frac{TU}{RS}$. You should find that $\frac{AB}{BC} \approx \frac{PQ}{QR}$ and $\frac{EF}{CD} \approx \frac{TU}{RS}$. (The ratios may not be exactly equal because the measurements are not exact.) So, the ratio between two sides of polygon *ABCDEF* is the same as the ratio between the corresponding sides of *PQRSTU*.

The relationships you discovered in the investigation illustrate the mathematical definition of similar polygons.

Two polygons are **similar** if and only if the corresponding angles are congruent and the corresponding sides are proportional.

The statement *CORN ~ PEAS* says that quadrilateral *CORN* is similar to quadrilateral *PEAS*. The order of the letters tells you which sides and angles correspond.

Look at quadrilaterals *SQUE* and *RCTL* on page 583 of your book. These figures have congruent corresponding angles, but they are *not* similar because the corresponding sides are *not* proportional.

(continued)

Now look at quadrilaterals *SQUE* and *RHOM*. These figures have corresponding sides that are proportional, but they are *not* similar because the corresponding angles are *not* congruent.

These examples illustrate that for two figures to be similar, both conditions—proportional sides and congruent angles—must hold. Here is another example.

**EXAMPLE** | Determine whether parallelogram *MNOP* is similar to parallelogram *WXYZ*.

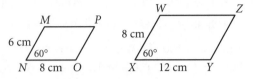

▶ **Solution** | $m\angle N = m\angle X$. Using angle properties of parallelograms, $m\angle M = m\angle W = 120°$, $m\angle P = m\angle Z = 60°$, and $m\angle O = m\angle Y = 120°$. So, the corresponding angles are congruent.

However, because $\frac{MN}{WX} = \frac{6}{8} = \frac{3}{4}$ and $\frac{NO}{XY} = \frac{8}{12} = \frac{2}{3}$, the corresponding sides are not proportional. Therefore, the parallelograms are not similar.

If you know that two polygons are similar, you can use the definition of similar polygons to find missing measures. The example in your book shows you how. Read this example carefully and make sure you understand it.

In Chapter 7, you saw that rigid transformations—translations, rotations, and reflections—preserve the size and shape of a figure, resulting in an image that is congruent to the original. In the next investigation you will look at a nonrigid transformation called a **dilation.**

## Investigation 2: Dilations on the Coordinate Plane

To *dilate* a figure in the coordinate plane about the origin, you multiply the coordinates of all its vertices by the same number, called a **scale factor.**

Pentagon *ABCDE* in your book has vertices with coordinates $A(-4, -4)$, $B(-2, 6)$, $C(4, 4)$, $D(6, -2)$, $E(0, -6)$. If you multiply each coordinate by $\frac{1}{2}$, you get $A'(-2, -2)$, $B'(-1, 3)$, $C'(2, 2)$, $D'(3, -1)$, $E'(0, -3)$. The figure at right shows the original pentagon and the image.

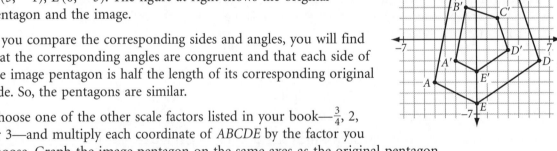

If you compare the corresponding sides and angles, you will find that the corresponding angles are congruent and that each side of the image pentagon is half the length of its corresponding original side. So, the pentagons are similar.

Choose one of the other scale factors listed in your book—$\frac{3}{4}$, 2, or 3—and multiply each coordinate of *ABCDE* by the factor you choose. Graph the image pentagon on the same axes as the original pentagon. Compare the corresponding angle measures and side lengths. Are the two pentagons similar? State your findings as a conjecture.

**Dilation Similarity Conjecture** If one polygon is a dilated image of another polygon, then _____.    `C-90`

# 11.2 Similar Triangles

In this lesson you will

- Learn **shortcuts** for determining whether two triangles are similar

In Lesson 11.1, you saw that to determine whether two quadrilaterals are congruent, you must check *both* that their corresponding sides are proportional *and* that their corresponding angles are congruent.

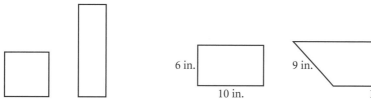

Angles are congruent, but
quadrilaterals are *not* similar.

Sides are proportional, but
quadrilaterals are *not* similar.

However, triangles are different. In Chapter 4, you discovered that you don't have to check every pair of sides and angles to determine whether two triangles are congruent. You found that SSS, SAS, ASA, and SAA are congruence shortcuts. In this lesson you will find that there are also similarity shortcuts.

Page 589 of your book shows two triangles in which only one pair of angles is congruent. The triangles are clearly not similar. So, knowing only that one pair of angles is congruent is not enough to conclude that two triangles are similar. What if two pairs of angles are congruent?

## Investigation 1: Is AA a Similarity Shortcut?

In the triangles at right, $\angle A \cong \angle D$ and $\angle B \cong \angle E$. What must be true about $\angle C$ and $\angle F$? Why?

Measure the sides and compare the ratios of corresponding side lengths. Is $\frac{AB}{DE} \approx \frac{AC}{DF} \approx \frac{BC}{EF}$?

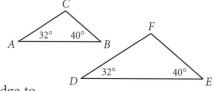

Now draw your own triangle *ABC*. Use a compass and straightedge to construct triangle *DEF*, with $\angle A \cong \angle D$ and $\angle B \cong \angle E$. Are your triangles similar? Explain.

Your findings should support this conjecture.

> **AA Similarity Conjecture** If two angles of one triangle are congruent to two angles of another triangle, then the triangles are similar.   **C-91**

Now consider similarity shortcuts that compare only corresponding sides. The illustration on page 590 of your book shows that you cannot conclude that two triangles are similar given that two pairs of corresponding sides are proportional. What if all three pairs of corresponding sides are proportional?

(continued)

### Investigation 2: Is SSS a Similarity Shortcut?

Use the segments on the left to construct △*ABC*. Each segment on the right is three times the length of the corresponding segment on the left. Use the segments on the right to construct △*DEF*.

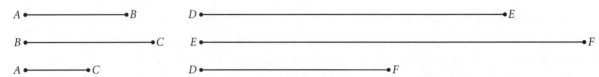

The side lengths of △*DEF* are proportional to the side lengths of △*ABC*. Measure the angles and see how they compare. Are the triangles similar?

Construct another pair of triangles so that the side lengths of one triangle are a multiple of the side lengths of the other. Compare the corresponding angles of your triangles.

You can now complete this conjecture.

> **SSS Similarity Conjecture** If the three sides of one triangle are proportional to the three sides of another triangle, then the two triangles are _____.    | **C-92**

If AA is a similarity shortcut, then so are ASA, SAA, and AAA, because each of those shortcuts contains two angles. That leaves SAS and SSA as possible shortcuts. In the next investigation you will look at SAS.

### Investigation 3: Is SAS a Similarity Shortcut?

Try to construct two different triangles that are *not* similar, but that have two pairs of sides proportional and the pair of included angles equal in measure. Can you do it? Your findings should support this conjecture.

> **SAS Similarity Conjecture** If two sides of one triangle are proportional to two sides of another triangle and the included angles are congruent, then the triangles are similar.    | **C-93**

In the triangles below, two pairs of corresponding sides are proportional and one pair of non-included angles is congruent. However, the triangles are clearly not similar. This shows that SSA is *not* a similarity shortcut.

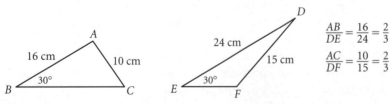

$$\frac{AB}{DE} = \frac{16}{24} = \frac{2}{3}$$

$$\frac{AC}{DF} = \frac{10}{15} = \frac{2}{3}$$

$\frac{AB}{DE} = \frac{AC}{DF}$ and $\angle B \cong \angle E$, but the triangles are not similar.

# Indirect Measurement with Similar Triangles

**CONDENSED**
**LESSON**
**11.3**

In this lesson you will

- Learn how to use similar triangles to measure tall objects and large distances **indirectly**

Suppose you want to find the height of a tall object such as a flagpole. It would be difficult to measure the flagpole directly—you would need a very tall ladder and a very long tape measure! In this lesson you will learn how you can use similar triangles to find the heights of tall objects indirectly.

## Investigation: Mirror, Mirror

You will need another person to help you with this investigation. You will also need a small mirror, a meterstick, and masking tape.

Mark crosshairs on your mirror with masking tape or a soluble pen. Label the intersection point *X*.

Choose a tall object, such as a flagpole, a tall tree, a basketball hoop, or a tall building.

Set the mirror, faceup, on the ground several yards from the object you wish to measure.

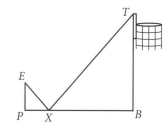

Step back from the mirror, staying in line with the mirror and the object, until you see the reflection of the top of the object at point *X* on the mirror.

Have another person measure and record the distances from you to *X* and from *X* to the base of the object. Also, have the person measure and record your height at eye level.

Sketch a diagram of your setup, like this one. Label the top of the object *T*, the base of the object *B*, the point where you stood *P*, and your eye level *E*. Label $\overline{PX}$, $\overline{BX}$, and $\overline{EP}$ with the measurements your helper found.

Think of $\overline{TX}$ as the path of a light ray that bounced back to your eye along $\overline{XE}$. Because the incoming angle must be congruent to the outgoing angle, $\angle EXP \cong \angle TXB$. Also, because $\overline{EP}$ and $\overline{TB}$ are perpendicular to the ground, $\angle P \cong \angle B$. By the AA Similarity Conjecture, $\triangle EPX \sim \triangle TBX$.

Because the triangles are similar, you can set up a proportion to find *TB*, the height of the tall object.

$$\frac{EP}{PX} = \frac{TB}{BX}$$

Find the height of your object. Then write a paragraph summarizing your work. Discuss possible causes of error.

(continued)

## Lesson 11.3 • Indirect Measurement with Similar Triangles (continued)

The example in your book illustrates a method of indirect measurement that involves shadows. Read the example and make sure you can explain why the two triangles are similar. Here is another example.

**EXAMPLE**  A brick building casts a shadow 7 feet long. At the same time, a 3-foot-tall child casts a shadow 6 inches long. How tall is the building?

▶ **Solution**  The drawing below shows the similar triangles formed. Find $x$ by setting up and solving a proportion.

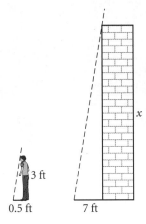

0.5 ft    7 ft

$$\frac{\text{Height of child}}{\text{Length of child's shadow}} = \frac{\text{Height of building}}{\text{Length of building's shadow}}$$

$$\frac{3}{0.5} = \frac{x}{7}$$

$$6 = \frac{x}{7}$$

$$7 \cdot 6 = x$$

$$42 = x$$

The building is 42 feet tall.

*Discovering Geometry Condensed Lessons*
©2008 Key Curriculum Press

# Corresponding Parts of Similar Triangles

In this lesson you will

- Investigate the relationship between **corresponding altitudes, corresponding medians,** and **corresponding angle bisectors** of similar triangles
- **Prove** that the lengths of corresponding medians of similar triangles are proportional to the lengths of corresponding sides
- Discover a **proportional relationship involving angle bisectors**

If two triangles are similar, then their side lengths are proportional. In the next investigation you will see if there is a relationship between the lengths of corresponding altitudes, corresponding medians, or corresponding angle bisectors.

## Investigation 1: Corresponding Parts

$\triangle PQR \sim \triangle DEF$. The scale factor from $\triangle PQR$ to $\triangle DEF$ is $\frac{3}{4}$.

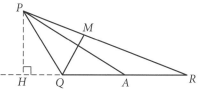
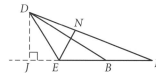

$\overline{PH}$ and $\overline{DJ}$ are corresponding altitudes. How do the lengths of these altitudes compare? How does the comparison relate to the scale factor?

$\overline{PA}$ and $\overline{DB}$ are corresponding medians. How do the lengths of these medians compare?

$\overline{QM}$ and $\overline{EN}$ are corresponding angle bisectors. How do the lengths of these angle bisectors compare?

Now draw your own triangle and then construct a similar triangle of a different size. Tell what scale factor you used. Follow Steps 2–4 in your book to construct and compare the lengths of corresponding altitudes, medians, and angle bisectors.

Summarize your findings in this investigation by completing the conjecture below.

> **Proportional Parts Conjecture** If two triangles are similar, then the                    **C-94**
> lengths of the corresponding _____, _____,
> and _____ are _____ to the lengths of the
> corresponding sides.

(continued)

**Lesson 11.4 • Corresponding Parts of Similar Triangles (continued)**

If a triangle is isosceles, the bisector of the vertex angle divides the opposite sides into equal parts. (That is, the angle bisector is also a median.) However, as the triangle on the right below shows, this is not true for all triangles.

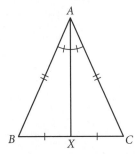

$\overline{AX}$ is an angle bisector.
Point $X$ is the midpoint of $\overline{BC}$.

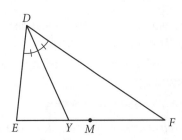

$\overline{DY}$ is an angle bisector.
Point $M$ is the midpoint of $\overline{EF}$.

The angle bisector does, however, divide the opposite side in a particular way.

**Investigation 2: Opposite Side Ratios**

Follow Steps 1–5 in your book.

You should find that both ratios are equal to $\frac{1}{2}$.

Repeat Steps 1–5 in your book with $AC = 6$ units and $AB = 18$ units.

This time you should find that $\frac{CA}{BA}$ and $\frac{CD}{BD}$ are both equal to $\frac{1}{3}$.

You can state your findings as a conjecture.

> **Angle Bisector/Opposite Side Conjecture** A bisector of an angle in a triangle divides the opposite side into two segments whose lengths are in the same ratio as the lengths of the two sides forming the angle.
>
> **C-95**

The example in your book proves that in similar triangles, the lengths of the corresponding medians are proportional to the lengths of corresponding sides. Read the example, following along with each step of the proof.

*Discovering Geometry Condensed Lessons*
©2008 Key Curriculum Press

# Proportions with Area

In this lesson you will

- Discover the **relationship between the areas** of similar figures

How does multiplying the dimensions of a two-dimensional figure by a scale factor affect its area? In this lesson you will explore this question.

## Investigation 1: Area Ratios

The rectangle on the right was created by multiplying the side lengths of the rectangle on the left by 3.

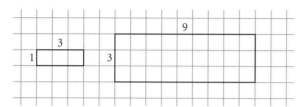

The area of the small rectangle is 3 square units. The area of the large rectangle is 27 square units. The ratio of side lengths of the larger rectangle to side lengths of the smaller rectangle is $\frac{3}{1}$, and the ratio of areas is $\frac{9}{1}$. Notice that nine copies of the small rectangle fit inside the large rectangle.

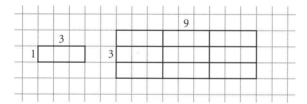

Now draw your own rectangle on graph paper. Then create a larger or smaller rectangle by multiplying the sides by a scale factor other than 3. What is the ratio of side lengths of the larger rectangle to side lengths of the smaller rectangle? What is the ratio of the areas? How do the two ratios compare?

Draw a triangle on graph paper (your work will be easiest if you draw a right triangle). Draw a similar triangle by multiplying the side lengths by a scale factor. Find the ratio of side lengths and the ratio of areas. How do the ratios compare?

Do you think your findings would be the same for any pair of polygons?

Would your findings be the same for a circle? Consider a circle with radius 5 cm and a circle with radius 20 cm. How does the ratio of radii compare to the ratio of areas?

(continued)

The following conjecture summarizes the relationship between the areas of similar figures.

---

**Proportional Areas Conjecture** If corresponding side lengths of two similar polygons or the radii of two circles compare in the ratio $\frac{m}{n}$, then their areas compare in the ratio $\frac{m^2}{n^2}$.

C-96

---

The reason behind the Proportional Areas Conjecture is that area is a two-dimensional measure. Calculating area involves multiplying two linear measures, such as base and height. So, if a rectangle has base $b$ and height $h$, then its area is $bh$. If the base and height are each multiplied by 2, then the area of the new rectangle is $2b \cdot 2h$, or $4bh$. This is four times the area of the original rectangle. Similarly, if the base and height are each multiplied by 3, then the area of the new rectangle is $3b \cdot 3h$, or $9bh$. This is nine times the area of the original rectangle.

## Investigation 2: Surface Area Ratios

In this investigation you will explore whether the Proportional Areas Conjecture is true for surface areas of similar figures. For this investigation you will need interlocking cubes and isometric dot paper.

Follow Steps 1–3 in your book.

You should find that the surface area for the Step 1 figure is 22 square units, while the surface area for a similar prism enlarged by the scale factor 2 is 88 square units. So, lengths of corresponding edges have ratio 2 to 1, while the ratio of the surface areas is 88 to 22, or 4 to 1.

Follow Step 4 in your book. Make sure you include the area of every face, including the face that the figure is resting on.

You should find that the surface area of the figure is 28 square units.

Follow Steps 5 and 6 in your book.

If your answers for Steps 5 and 6 are correct, you can correctly conclude that the Proportional Areas Conjecture also applies to surface area.

---

The example in your book shows how to use the Proportional Areas Conjecture to solve a real-life problem. Solve the problem yourself before reading the solution.

# Proportions with Volume

In this lesson you will

- Discover the **relationship between the volumes** of similar solids

How does multiplying every dimension of a three-dimensional solid by the same scale factor affect its volume? In this lesson you will explore this question.

Suppose you are going to create a statue that is 2 feet high. You first create a smaller version of the statue that is 4 inches tall and weighs 8 ounces. How much clay should you buy for the larger statue? Would you believe you'll need 108 pounds of clay? When you finish this lesson, you'll understand why.

**Similar solids** are solids that have the same shape, but not necessarily the same size. All cubes are similar, but not all prisms are similar. All spheres are similar, but not all cylinders are similar. Two polyhedrons are similar if all their corresponding faces are similar and the lengths of their corresponding edges are proportional. Two right cylinders or right cones are similar if their radii and heights are proportional.

Examples A and B in your book involve determining whether two given solids are similar. Try to answer the problems yourself before reading the solutions.

Here is another example.

**EXAMPLE** | Are these two right cylinders similar?

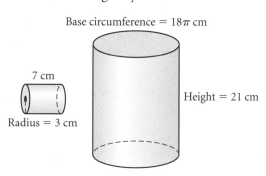

Base circumference = $18\pi$ cm

7 cm

Radius = 3 cm

Height = 21 cm

▶ **Solution** | Find the radius of the larger cylinder.

$$C = 2\pi r$$

$$18\pi = 2\pi r$$

$$r = 9$$

The radius is 9 cm.

Comparing the lengths of corresponding parts we see:

The ratio of the radii is $\frac{3}{9} = \frac{1}{3}$.

The ratio of the heights is $\frac{7}{21} = \frac{1}{3}$.

The radii and heights are proportional, so the right cylinders are similar.

(continued)

## Investigation: Volume Ratios

In this investigation you'll explore how the ratio of the edge lengths of similar solids compares to the ratio of the volumes. You will need interlocking cubes and isometric dot paper.

Follow Steps 1 and 2 in your book. In Step 2, make sure you multiply all three dimensions—length, width, and height—by 2.

What is the ratio of the side lengths (larger to smaller) for the two "snakes"? What is the ratio of the volumes? How do the ratios compare?

Follow Steps 4–6 in your book. How would the volume change if you multiplied each dimension by 5? By $\frac{1}{2}$?

Your findings can be stated as a conjecture.

---

**Proportional Volumes Conjecture** If corresponding edge lengths (or radii, or heights) of two similar solids compare in the ratio $\frac{m}{n}$, then their volumes compare in the ratio $\frac{m^3}{n^3}$. C-97

---

The example in your book shows how to apply both the Proportional Areas Conjecture and the Proportional Volumes Conjecture. Work through the example to understand how each conjecture is used. Then read the example below. Solve the problem yourself before reading the solution.

**EXAMPLE**  A "square can" is a right cylinder that has a height equal to its diameter. One square can has height 5 cm and another has height 12 cm. About how many full cans of water from the smaller can are needed to fill the larger can?

**Solution**  The ratio of the radius of the larger can to the radius of the smaller can is $\frac{6}{2.5} = \frac{12}{5}$, which is the same as the ratio of the heights. So, the two square cans are similar.

The amount of water needed to fill each can is determined by the volume of the can, so find the ratio of the volumes. The ratio of the heights is $\frac{12}{5}$. Therefore, the ratio of the volumes is $\frac{12^3}{5^3}$, or $\frac{1728}{125}$.

$\frac{1728}{125} \approx 13.8$, so it takes almost 14 cans of water from the smaller can to fill the larger can.

# Proportional Segments Between Parallel Lines

In this lesson you will

- Explore the relationships in the lengths of segments formed when one or more lines parallel to one side of a triangle intersect the other two sides
- Learn how you can use the relationship you discover to divide a given segment into any number of equal parts

The top of page 623 in your book shows $\triangle LUV$ and line $MT$, with $\overrightarrow{MT} \parallel \overline{LU}$. It appears that $\triangle LUV \sim \triangle MTV$. The paragraph proof given uses the AA Similarity Conjecture to prove this is true. Example A in your book uses the similarity of two triangles to solve a problem. Read the example, and follow along with each step in the solution.

Look at the figure from Example A. Notice that $\frac{LE}{EM} = \frac{45}{60} = \frac{3}{4}$ and $\frac{NO}{OM} = \frac{36}{48} = \frac{3}{4}$, so there are more relationships in the figure than the ones found by using similar triangles. You will explore these relationships in the next investigation.

## Investigation 1: Parallels and Proportionality

Step 1 of the investigation gives three triangles, each with a line parallel to one side that intersects the other two sides. For each triangle, find $x$ and then find the values of the specified ratios. Here is the solution to part a.

**a.** Use the fact that $\triangle CDE \sim \triangle BDA$ to write and solve a proportion.

$$\frac{DE}{DA} = \frac{DC}{DB}$$      Corresponding parts of similar triangles are proportional.

$$\frac{8}{24} = \frac{12}{12 + x}$$      Substitute the lengths from the figure.

$$\frac{1}{3} = \frac{12}{12 + x}$$      Simplify the left side.

$$\frac{1(3)(12 + x)}{3} = \frac{12(3)(12 + x)}{12 + x}$$      Multiply both sides by $3(12 + x)$.

$$12 + x = 36$$      Simplify.

$$x = 24$$      Subtract 12 from both sides.

So, $\frac{DE}{AE} = \frac{8}{16} = \frac{1}{2}$ and $\frac{DC}{BC} = \frac{12}{24} = \frac{1}{2}$.

In each part of Step 1, you should find that the ratios of the lengths of the segments cut by the parallel line are equal. In other words: If a line parallel to one side of a triangle passes through the other two sides, then it divides the other two sides proportionally.

Do you think the converse of this statement is also true? That is, if a line divides two sides of a triangle proportionally, is it parallel to the third side?

Follow Steps 3–7 in your book. You should find that $\angle PAC \cong \angle PBD$, so $\overline{AC}$ and $\overline{BD}$ are parallel.

Repeat Steps 3–7, but this time mark off your own lengths, such that $\frac{PA}{AB} = \frac{PC}{CD}$. Again, you should find that $\overline{AC}$ is parallel to $\overline{BD}$. You can use your findings from this investigation to state a conjecture.

(continued)

> **Parallel/Proportionality Conjecture** If a line parallel to one side of a triangle passes through the other two sides, then it divides the other two sides proportionally. Conversely, if a line cuts two sides of a triangle proportionally, then it is parallel to the third side. **C-98**

Example B proves the first part of the Parallel/Proportionality Conjecture. Write a proof yourself before reading the one in the book. Use the fact that $\triangle AXY \sim \triangle ABC$ to set up a proportion. Then write a series of algebraic steps until you get $\frac{a}{c} = \frac{b}{d}$.

## Investigation 2: Extended Parallel/Proportionality

In the triangles in Step 1, more than one segment is drawn parallel to one side of a triangle. Find the missing lengths. Here is the solution to part a. To find $x$ and $y$, apply the Parallel/Proportionality Conjecture to the appropriate triangles and lines.

**a.** To find $x$, use $\triangle AEL$ and $\overline{FT}$.

$$\frac{EF}{FL} = \frac{ET}{TA}$$

$$\frac{21}{35} = \frac{42}{x}$$

$$x = 70$$

To find $y$, use $\triangle REG$ and $\overline{LA}$.

$$\frac{EL}{LG} = \frac{EA}{AR}$$

$$\frac{56}{28} = \frac{112}{y}$$

$$y = 56$$

Using the values of $x$ and $y$, you can see that $\frac{FL}{LG} = \frac{TA}{AR} = \frac{5}{4}$.

The results of Step 1 lead to the following conjecture.

> **Extended Parallel/Proportionality Conjecture** If two or more lines pass through two sides of a triangle parallel to the third side, then they divide the two sides proportionally. **C-99**

You can use the Extended Parallel/Proportionality Conjecture to divide a segment into any number of equal parts. Example C in your book shows you how to divide a segment, $AB$, into three equal parts. Read the example carefully. To make sure you understand the process, divide $\overline{XY}$ below into three equal parts using a compass and straightedge.

$X \bullet$ _____ $\bullet Y$

# 12.1 Trigonometric Ratios

In this lesson you will

- Learn about the trigonometric ratios **sine, cosine,** and **tangent**
- Use trigonometric ratios to **find unknown side lengths** in right triangles
- Use **inverse trigonometric functions** to **find unknown angle measures** in right triangles

Read up to Example A in your book. Your book explains that, in any right triangle with an acute angle of a given measure, the ratio of the length of the leg opposite the angle to the length of the leg adjacent to the angle is the same. The ratio is known as the **tangent** of the angle. Example A uses the fact that $\tan 31° \approx \frac{3}{5}$ to solve a problem. Read the example carefully.

In addition to tangent, mathematicians have named five other ratios relating the side lengths of right triangles. In this book, you will work with three ratios: **sine, cosine,** and **tangent,** abbreviated sin, cos, and tan. These ratios are defined on pages 641–642 of your book.

## Investigation: Trigonometric Tables

Measure the side lengths of $\triangle ABC$ to the nearest millimeter. Then use the side lengths and the definitions of sine, cosine, and tangent to fill in the "First $\triangle$" row of the table. Express the ratios as decimals to the nearest thousandth.

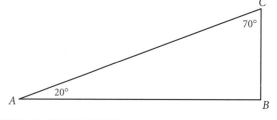

| | $m\angle A$ | sin A | cos A | tan A | $m\angle C$ | sin C | cos C | tan C |
|---|---|---|---|---|---|---|---|---|
| **First △** | 20° | | | | 70° | | | |
| **Second △** | 20° | | | | 70° | | | |
| **Average** | — | | | | — | | | |

Now use your protractor to draw a different right triangle $ABC$, with $m\angle A = 20°$ and $m\angle C = 70°$. Measure the sides to the nearest millimeter and fill in the "Second $\triangle$" row of the table.

Calculate the average for each ratio and put the results in the last row of the table. Look for patterns in your table. You should find that $\sin 20° = \cos 70°$ and $\sin 70° = \cos 20°$. Notice also that $\tan 20° = \frac{1}{\tan 70°}$ and $\tan 70° = \frac{1}{\tan 20°}$. Use the definitions of sine, cosine, and tangent to explain why these relationships exist.

You can use your calculator to find the sine, cosine, or tangent of any angle. Experiment with your calculator until you figure out how to do this. Then use your calculator to find $\sin 20°$, $\cos 20°$, $\tan 20°$, $\sin 70°$, $\cos 70°$, and $\tan 70°$. Compare the results to the ratios you found by measuring sides.

*(continued)*

## Lesson 12.1 • Trigonometric Ratios (continued)

You can use trigonometric ratios to find unknown side lengths of a right triangle given the measures of any side and any acute angle. Read Example B in your book and then read Example A below.

**EXAMPLE A** | Find the value of *x*.

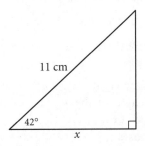

▶ **Solution** | You need to find the length of the leg adjacent to the 42° angle. You are given the length of the hypotenuse. The trigonometric ratio that relates the adjacent leg and the hypotenuse is the cosine ratio.

$$\cos 42° = \frac{x}{11}$$

$11 \cdot \cos 42° = x$     Multiply both sides by 11.

$8.17 \approx x$     Use your calculator to find cos 42° and multiply the result by 11.

The value of *x* is about 8.2 cm.

If you know the lengths of any two sides of a right triangle, you can use *inverse trigonometric functions* to find the angle measures. Example C in your book shows how to use the inverse tangent, or $\tan^{-1}$, function. The example below uses the inverse sine, or $\sin^{-1}$, function.

**EXAMPLE B** | Find the measure of the angle opposite the 32-inch leg.

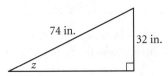

▶ **Solution** | You are given the lengths of the leg opposite the angle and the hypotenuse. The ratio that relates these lengths is the sine ratio.

$$\sin z = \frac{32}{74}$$

$\sin^{-1}(\sin z) = \sin^{-1}\left(\frac{32}{74}\right)$     Take the inverse sine of both sides.

$z = \sin^{-1}\left(\frac{32}{74}\right)$     The inverse sine function undoes the sine function.

$z \approx 25.6°$     Use your calculator to find $\sin^{-1}\left(\frac{32}{74}\right)$.

The measure of the angle opposite the 32-inch side is about 26°.

*Discovering Geometry Condensed Lessons*
©2008 Key Curriculum Press

# Problem Solving with Right Triangles

In this lesson you will

- Use trigonometry to **solve problems involving right triangles**

Right triangle trigonometry is often used to find the height of a tall object indirectly. To solve a problem of this type, measure the angle from the horizontal to your line of sight when you look at the top or bottom of the object.

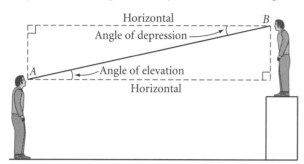

If you look up, you measure the **angle of elevation.** If you look down, you measure the **angle of depression.**

The example in your book uses the angle of elevation to find a distance indirectly. Read the example carefully. Try to solve the problem on your own before reading the solution. Then try to solve the problems in the examples below. Example A is Exercise 13 in your book. It involves an angle of depression.

**EXAMPLE A** | A salvage ship's sonar locates wreckage at a 12° angle of depression. A diver is lowered 40 meters to the ocean floor. How far does the diver need to walk along the ocean floor to the wreckage?

▶ **Solution** | Make a sketch to illustrate the situation. Notice that because the ocean floor is parallel to the surface of the water, the angle of elevation from the wreckage to the ship is equal to the angle of depression from the ship to the wreckage (by the AIA Conjecture).

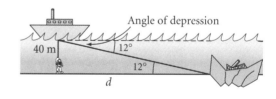

The distance the diver is lowered (40 m) is the length of the leg opposite the 12° angle. The distance the diver must walk is the length of the leg adjacent to the 12° angle. Set up the tangent ratio.

$$\tan 12° = \frac{40}{d}$$

$$d\tan 12° = 40$$

$$d = \frac{40}{\tan 12°}$$

$$d \approx 188.19$$

The diver must walk approximately 188 meters to reach the wreckage.

(continued)

**EXAMPLE B** | An evergreen tree is supported by a wire extending from 1.5 feet below the top of the tree to a stake in the ground. The wire is 24 feet long and forms a 58° angle with the ground. How tall is the tree?

▶ **Solution** | Make a sketch to illustrate the situation.

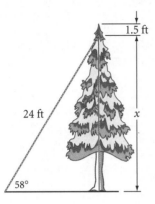

The length of the hypotenuse is given, and the unknown distance is the length of the side opposite the 58° angle. Set up the sine ratio.

$$\sin 58° = \frac{x}{24}$$

$$24 \cdot \sin 58° = x$$

$$20.4 \approx x$$

The distance from the ground to the point where the wire is attached to the tree is about 20.4 feet. Because the wire is attached 1.5 feet from the top of the tree, the tree's height is about 20.4 + 1.5, or 21.9 feet.

# 12.3 The Law of Sines

In this lesson you will

- Find the **area of a triangle** when you know two side lengths and the measure of the included angle
- Derive the **Law of Sines,** which relates the side lengths of a triangle to the sines of the angle measures
- **Use the Law of Sines to find an unknown side length** of a triangle when you know the measures of two angles and one side **or to find an unknown** *acute* **angle measure** when you know the measures of two sides and one angle

You have used trigonometry to solve problems involving right triangles. In the next two lessons you will see that you can use trigonometry with *any* triangle.

Example A in your book gives the lengths of two sides of a triangle and the measure of the included angle and shows you how to find the area. Read the example carefully. In the next investigation you will generalize the method used in the example.

## Investigation 1: Area of a Triangle

Step 1 gives three triangles with the lengths of two sides and the measure of the included angle labeled. Use Example A as a guide to find the area of each triangle. Here is a solution to part b.

**b.** First find *h*.

$$\sin 72° = \frac{h}{21}$$

$$21 \cdot \sin 72° = h$$

Now find the area.

$$A = 0.5bh$$

$$A = 0.5(38.5)(21 \cdot \sin 72°)$$

$$A \approx 384.46$$

The area is about 384 cm².

Then use the triangle shown in Step 2 to derive a general formula. The conjecture below summarizes the results.

---

**SAS Triangle Area Conjecture** The area of a triangle is given by the formula $A = \frac{1}{2}ab \sin C$, where *a* and *b* are the lengths of two sides and *C* is the angle between them.  **C-100**

---

(continued)

## Lesson 12.3 • The Law of Sines (continued)

You can use what you've learned to derive the property called the Law of Sines.

### Investigation 2: The Law of Sines

Complete Steps 1–3 in your book. Below are the results you should find.

**Step 1**  $\sin B = \dfrac{h}{a}$, so $h = a \sin B$

**Step 2**  $\sin A = \dfrac{h}{b}$, so $h = b \sin A$

**Step 3**  Because both $b \sin A$ and $a \sin B$ are equal to $h$, you can set them equal to one another.

$b \sin A = a \sin B$

$\dfrac{b \sin A}{ab} = \dfrac{a \sin B}{ab}$  Divide both sides by $ab$.

$\dfrac{\sin A}{a} = \dfrac{\sin B}{b}$  Simplify.

Now complete Steps 4–6. Combine Steps 3 and 6 to get this conjecture.

---

**Law of Sines**  For a triangle with angles $A$, $B$, and $C$ and sides of lengths $a$, $b$, and $c$ ($a$ opposite $A$, $b$ opposite $B$, and $c$ opposite $C$), $\dfrac{\sin A}{a} = \dfrac{\sin B}{b} = \dfrac{\sin C}{c}$.

`C-101`

---

Example B in your book shows you how to use the Law of Sines to find the lengths of a triangle's sides when you know one side length and two angle measures. Try to solve the problem yourself before reading the solution.

Read the text before Example C, which explains that you can use the Law of Sines to find the measure of a missing angle *only if* you know whether the angle is acute or obtuse. You will only be asked to find acute angle measures. Example C shows you how to do this. Here is another example.

**EXAMPLE** | Find the measure of acute angle $C$.

▶ **Solution** | Use the Law of Sines.

$\dfrac{\sin A}{a} = \dfrac{\sin C}{c}$

$\sin C = \dfrac{c \sin A}{a}$

$\sin C = \dfrac{48 \sin 72°}{60}$

$C = \sin^{-1}\left(\dfrac{48 \sin 72°}{60}\right)$

$C \approx 49.54$

The measure of $\angle C$ is approximately 50°.

# The Law of Cosines

In this lesson you will

- Use the **Law of Cosines** to find side lengths and angle measures in a triangle

You have solved many problems by using the Pythagorean Theorem. The Pythagorean Theorem is a very powerful problem-solving tool, but it is limited to right triangles. There is a more general relationship that applies to all triangles.

Think of a right angle that is made by a hinge with two legs of fixed length as its sides. What happens to the length of the third side (the hypotenuse when the angle measures 90°) and to the Pythagorean relationship as the hinge closes to less than a right angle or opens to more than a right angle? To explore this question, look at the triangles pictured at the top of page 661 and read the paragraphs that follow, including the Law of Cosines. Add the Law of Cosines to your conjecture list.

The Law of Cosines works for both acute and obtuse triangles. In your book, read the derivation of the Law of Cosines for acute triangles on page 662. In Example A, the Law of Cosines is used to find the length of the third side of a triangle when you are given the lengths of two sides and the measure of their included angle. Read Example A in your book. Then work through Example A below.

**EXAMPLE A** | Find $m$, the length of side $\overline{NL}$ in acute $\triangle LMN$.

▶ **Solution** | Use the Law of Cosines and solve for $m$.

$c^2 = a^2 + b^2 - 2ab \cos C$      The Law of Cosines.

$m^2 = 96^2 + 84^2 - 2(96)(84)(\cos 77°)$      Substitute $m$ for $c$, 96 for $a$, 84 for $b$, and 77° for $C$.

$m = \sqrt{96^2 + 84^2 - 2(96)(84)(\cos 77°)}$      Take the positive square root of both sides.

$m \approx 112.45$      Evaluate.

The length of side $\overline{NL}$ is about 112 cm.

(continued)

# Lesson 12.4 • The Law of Cosines (continued)

Example B in your book uses the Law of Cosines to find an angle measure.
Here is another example. Solve the problem yourself before reading the solution.

**EXAMPLE B**  | Find the measure of $\angle I$ in $\triangle TRI$.

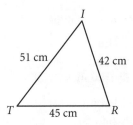

▶ **Solution** | Use the Law of Cosines and solve for $I$.

$$c^2 = a^2 + b^2 - 2ab \cos C$$  The Law of Cosines.

$$45^2 = 51^2 + 42^2 - 2(51)(42)(\cos I)$$  Substitute 45 for $c$, 51 for $a$, 42 for $b$, and $I$ for $C$.

$$\cos I = \frac{45^2 - 51^2 - 42^2}{-2(51)(42)}$$  Solve for $\cos I$.

$$I = \cos^{-1}\left(\frac{45^2 - 51^2 - 42^2}{-2(51)(42)}\right)$$  Take the inverse cosine of both sides.

$$I \approx 56.89$$  Evaluate.

The measure of $\angle I$ is about 57°.

*Discovering Geometry Condensed Lessons*
©2008 Key Curriculum Press

# Problem Solving with Trigonometry

In this lesson you will

- Use trigonometry to solve problems, including problems that involve **vectors**

Some of the practical applications of trigonometry involve vectors. In earlier vector activities, you used a ruler and a protractor to measure the size of the resulting vector and the angle between vectors. Now you will be able to calculate resulting vectors by using the Law of Sines and the Law of Cosines.

In the example in your book, the Law of Cosines is used to find the length of a resultant vector and the Law of Sines is used to find its direction. Read the example and make sure you understand each step.

The example below is Exercise 5 in your book. Try to solve the problem on your own before reading the solution.

**EXAMPLE**  Annie and Sashi are backpacking in the Sierra Nevada. They walk 8 km from their base camp at a bearing of 42°. After lunch, they change direction to a bearing of 137° and walk another 5 km.

**a.** How far are Annie and Sashi from their base camp?

**b.** At what bearing must Sashi and Annie travel to return to their base camp?

▶ **Solution**  **a.** Draw a diagram to illustrate the situation. (Remember, a bearing is measured clockwise from north.) Here, the distance from base camp is $r$. To find $r$, you can find the value of $\theta$ and then use the Law of Cosines.

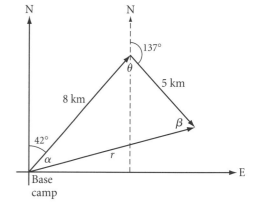

Think of $\theta$ as being made up of two parts, the part to the left of the vertical and the part to the right. Using the AIA Conjecture, the part to the left has measure 42°. Because the part to the right and the 137° angle are a linear pair, the part to the right has measure 43°. So, the measure of $\theta$ is 42° + 43°, or 85°. Now use the Law of Cosines.

$$r^2 = 8^2 + 5^2 - 2(8)(5)(\cos 85°)$$

$$r = \sqrt{8^2 + 5^2 - 2(8)(5)(\cos 85°)}$$

$$r \approx 9.06$$

Sashi and Annie are about 9.1 km from their base camp.

(continued)

**b.** Add the information you found in part a to the diagram.

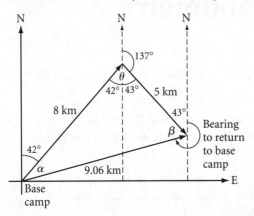

The diagram indicates that the bearing Sashi and Annie must travel to return to the base camp is $360° - (43° + \beta)$. To find $\beta$, use the Law of Sines.

$$\frac{\sin\beta}{8} \approx \frac{\sin 85°}{9.06}$$

$$\sin\beta \approx \frac{8 \sin 85°}{9.06}$$

$$\beta \approx \sin^{-1}\left(\frac{8 \sin 85°}{9.06}\right)$$

$$\beta \approx 61.6$$

$\beta$ is about 62°, so the bearing is about $360° - (43° + 62°)$, or 255°.

# 13.1 The Premises of Geometry

In this lesson you will

- Learn about Euclid's **deductive system** for organizing geometry properties
- Become familiar with the four types of premises for geometry

Beginning in about 600 B.C.E., mathematicians began to use logical reasoning to deduce mathematical ideas. The Greek mathematician Euclid (ca. 325–265 B.C.E.) created a **deductive system** to organize geometry properties. He started with a simple collection of statements called **postulates.** He considered these postulates to be obvious truths that did not need to be proved. Euclid then systematically demonstrated how each geometry discovery followed logically from his postulates and his previously proved conjectures, or **theorems.**

Up to now, you have used informal proofs to explain why certain conjectures are true. However, you often relied on unproved conjectures in your proofs. A conclusion in a proof is true if and only if your premises are true and all of your arguments are valid.

In this chapter you will look at geometry as Euclid did. You will start with premises and systematically prove your earlier conjectures. Once you have proved a conjecture, it becomes a theorem that you can use to prove other conjectures. Read the four types of premises on page 693 of your book.

You are already familiar with the first type of premise. You have learned the undefined terms—point, line, and plane—and you have a list of definitions in your notebook.

The second type of premise is the properties of arithmetic, equality, and congruence. Read through the properties of arithmetic and equality in your book. You have used these properties many times to solve algebraic equations. The example in your book shows the solution to an algebraic equation, along with the reason for each step. This type of step-by-step solution is actually an algebraic proof. Here is another example.

**EXAMPLE** | Prove that if $(a + b)(a - b) = (a + b)(a + b)$ and $a + b \neq 0$, then $b = 0$.

**Solution** |

| | |
|---|---|
| $(a + b)(a - b) = (a + b)(a + b)$ | Given |
| $a - b = a + b$ | Division property of equality $(a + b \neq 0)$ |
| $a = a + 2b$ | Addition property of equality |
| $0 = 2b$ | Subtraction property of equality |
| $0 = b$ | Division property of equality |

Just as you use equality to express a relationship between numbers, you use congruence to express a relationship between geometric figures. Read the definition of congruence on page 695 of your book. Here are the properties of congruence.

(continued)

## Properties of Congruence

In the statements below, "figure" refers to a segment, an angle, or a geometric shape.

### Reflexive Property of Congruence

Any figure is congruent to itself.

### Transitive Property of Congruence

If Figure A ≅ Figure B and Figure B ≅ Figure C, then Figure A ≅ Figure C.

### Symmetric Property of Congruence

If Figure A ≅ Figure B, then Figure B ≅ Figure A.

The third type of premise is the postulates of geometry. Postulates are very basic statements that are useful and easy for everyone to agree on. Read the postulates of geometry on pages 696–697 of your book.

Some of the postulates allow you to add auxiliary lines, segments, and points to a diagram. For example, you can use the Line Postulate to construct a diagonal of a polygon, and you can use the Perpendicular Postulate to construct an altitude in a triangle.

Notice that the Corresponding Angles Conjecture and its converse are stated as a postulate, but the Alternate Interior Angles Conjecture is not. This means that you will need to prove the Alternate Interior Angles Conjecture before you can use it to prove other conjectures. Similarly, the SSS, SAS, and ASA Congruence Conjectures are stated as postulates, but SAA is not, so you will need to prove it.

The fourth type of premise is previously proved geometry conjectures, or theorems. Each time you prove a conjecture, you may rename it as a theorem and add it to your theorem list. You can use the theorems on your list to prove conjectures.

# 13.2 Planning a Geometry Proof

In this lesson you will

- Learn the **five tasks** involved in **writing a proof**
- Prove several conjectures about angles
- Learn how to create a **logical family tree** for a theorem

A proof in geometry is a sequence of statements, starting with a given set of premises and leading to a valid conclusion. Each statement must follow from previous statements and must be supported by a reason. The reason must come from the set of premises you learned about in Lesson 13.1.

Writing a proof involves five tasks.

Task 1 is to identify what is given and what is to be proved. This is easiest if the conjecture is a *conditional*, or "if-then," statement. The "if" part is what you are given, and the "then" part is what you must show. If a conjecture is not given this way, you can often restate it. For example, the conjecture "Vertical angles are congruent" can be rewritten as "If two angles are vertical angles, then they are congruent."

Task 2 is to make a diagram and to mark it so it illustrates the given information. Task 3 is to restate the "given" and "show" information in terms of the diagram. Task 4 is to make a plan for your proof, organizing your reasoning either mentally or on paper. Task 5 is to use your plan to write the proof. Page 703 of your book summarizes the five tasks involved in writing a proof.

A flowchart proof of the Vertical Angles Conjecture is given on page 704 of your book. Notice that the proof uses only postulates, definitions, and properties of equality. Thus, it is a valid proof. You can now call the conjecture the Vertical Angles (VA) Theorem and add it to your theorem list.

In Lesson 13.1, the Corresponding Angles (CA) Conjecture was stated as a postulate, but the Alternate Interior Angles (AIA) Conjecture was not. Example A in your book goes through the five-task process for proving the AIA Conjecture. Read the example carefully, and then add the AIA Theorem to your theorem list.

Example B proves the Triangle Sum Conjecture. The proof requires using the Parallel Postulate to construct a line parallel to one side of the triangle. After you read and understand the proof, add the Triangle Sum Theorem to your theorem list.

Pages 706–707 of your book give a proof of the Third Angle Conjecture. Read the proof, and then add the Third Angle Theorem to your theorem list.

A *logical family tree* for a theorem traces the theorem back to all the postulates on which the theorem relies. On page 707 of your book, you'll see how to construct the logical family tree for the Third Angle Theorem. Make sure you understand how this theorem is rooted in four postulates: the Parallel Postulate, the CA Postulate, the Linear Pair Postulate, and the Angle Addition Postulate.

On page 707 you can see that the Third Angle Theorem follows from the Triangle Sum Theorem without relying on any other postulate or theorem. A theorem that is an immediate consequence of another proven theorem is called a **corollary.** So, the Third Angle Theorem is a corollary of the Triangle Sum Theorem.

(continued)

The next example is Exercise 8 in your book. It illustrates the five-task process of proving the Converse of the Alternate Interior Angles Conjecture.

**EXAMPLE** | Prove the Converse of the AIA Conjecture: If two lines are cut by a transversal forming congruent alternate interior angles, then the lines are parallel. Then create a family tree for the Converse of the AIA Theorem.

▶ **Solution** | Task 1: Identify what is given and what you must show.

**Given:** Two lines cut by a transversal to form congruent alternate interior angles

**Show:** The lines are parallel

Task 2: Draw and label a diagram.

(*Note:* You may not realize that labeling ∠3 is useful until you make your plan.)

Task 3: Restate the given and show information in terms of your diagram.

**Given:** $\ell_1$ and $\ell_2$ cut by transversal $\ell_3$; ∠1 ≅ ∠2

**Show:** $\ell_1 \parallel \ell_2$

Task 4: Make a plan.

**Plan:** I need to prove that $\ell_1 \parallel \ell_2$. The only theorem or postulate I have for proving lines are parallel is the CA Postulate. If I can show that ∠1 ≅ ∠3, I can use the CA Postulate to conclude that $\ell_1 \parallel \ell_2$. I know that ∠1 ≅ ∠2. By the VA Theorem, ∠2 ≅ ∠3. So, by the transitive property of congruence, ∠1 ≅ ∠3.

Task 5: Create a proof.

**Flowchart Proof**

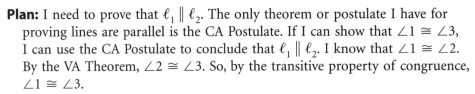

| ∠1 ≅ ∠2 | ∠2 ≅ ∠3 | ∠1 ≅ ∠3 | $\ell_1 \parallel \ell_2$ |
|---|---|---|---|
| Given | VA Theorem | Transitive property | CA Postulate |

Here is a logical family tree for the Converse of the AIA Theorem.

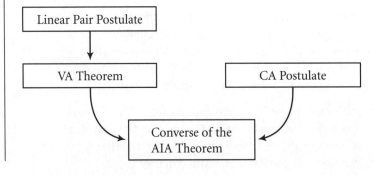

*Discovering Geometry Condensed Lessons*
©2008 Key Curriculum Press

# CONDENSED
# LESSON
# 13.3  Triangle Proofs

In this lesson you will

- Prove conjectures involving **properties of triangles**
- Learn how to write a **two-column proof**

In this lesson you will focus on triangle proofs. Read the lesson in your book. It takes you through the five-task process for proving the Angle Bisector Conjecture and explains how to write a **two-column proof.** The examples below are Exercises 1 and 2 in your book. For each example, write each proof yourself before reading the solution.

**EXAMPLE A**  Write a flowchart proof of the Perpendicular Bisector Conjecture: If a point is on the perpendicular bisector of a segment, then it is equally distant from the endpoints of the segment.

▸ **Solution**  Task 1: Identify what is given and what you must show.

**Given:**          A point on the perpendicular bisector of a segment

**Show:**          The point is equally distant from the endpoints of the segment

Task 2: Draw and label a diagram to illustrate the given information.

Task 3: Restate the given and show information in terms of the diagram.

**Given:**          $\overleftrightarrow{PQ}$ is the perpendicular bisector of $\overline{AB}$

**Show:**          $PA = PB$

Task 4: Plan a proof.

**Plan:** I can show that $PA = PB$ if $\overline{PA}$ and $\overline{PB}$ are corresponding parts of congruent triangles. I know that $\overline{AQ} \cong \overline{BQ}$ and $\angle PQA \cong \angle PQB$. I also know that $\overline{PQ} \cong \overline{PQ}$. Therefore, $\triangle PAQ \cong \triangle PBQ$ by the SAS Postulate. Thus, $\overline{PA} \cong \overline{PB}$ by CPCTC, so $PA = PB$.

Task 5: Write a proof based on your plan.

**Flowchart Proof**

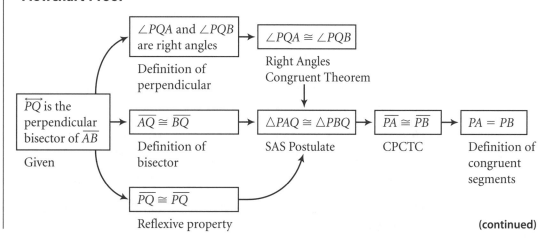

(continued)

**EXAMPLE B**   Write a two-column proof of the Converse of the Perpendicular Bisector Conjecture: If a point is equally distant from the endpoints of a segment, then it is on the perpendicular bisector of the segment.

▶ **Solution**   Task 1: Identify what is given and what you must show.

**Given:**   A point that is equally distant from the endpoints of a segment

**Show:**   The point is on the perpendicular bisector of the segment

Task 2: Draw and label a diagram to illustrate the given information.

Task 3: Restate the given and show information in terms of the diagram.

**Given:**   $PA = PB$

**Show:**   $P$ is on the perpendicular bisector of $\overline{AB}$

Task 4: Plan a proof.

I can start by constructing the midpoint $M$ of $\overline{AB}$ and $\overleftrightarrow{PM}$. I know that $\overleftrightarrow{PM}$ is a bisector of $\overline{AB}$, so I need only show that it is perpendicular to $\overline{AB}$. I can show that $\triangle PAM \cong \triangle PBM$ by SSS. Therefore, $\angle PMA \cong \angle PMB$. Because the angles form a linear pair, they are supplementary, so each has measure 90°. So, $\overleftrightarrow{PM} \perp \overline{AB}$.

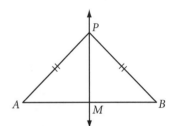

Task 5: Write a proof based on your plan.

| Statement | Reason |
|---|---|
| **1.** Construct the midpoint $M$ of $\overline{AB}$ | **1.** Midpoint Postulate |
| **2.** Construct $\overleftrightarrow{PM}$ | **2.** Line Postulate |
| **3.** $PA = PB$ | **3.** Given |
| **4.** $\overline{PA} \cong \overline{PB}$ | **4.** Definition of congruence |
| **5.** $\overline{AM} \cong \overline{BM}$ | **5.** Definition of midpoint |
| **6.** $\overline{PM} \cong \overline{PM}$ | **6.** Reflexive property of congruence |
| **7.** $\triangle PAM \cong \triangle PBM$ | **7.** SSS Postulate |
| **8.** $\angle PMA \cong \angle PMB$ | **8.** CPCTC |
| **9.** $\angle PMA$ and $\angle PMB$ are supplementary | **9.** Linear Pair Postulate |
| **10.** $\angle PMA$ and $\angle PMB$ are right angles | **10.** Congruent and Supplementary Theorem |
| **11.** $\overleftrightarrow{PM} \perp \overline{AB}$ | **11.** Definition of perpendicular |
| **12.** $\overleftrightarrow{PM}$ is the perpendicular bisector of $\overline{AB}$ | **12.** Definition of perpendicular bisector |

# 13.4 Quadrilateral Proofs

In this lesson you will

- Prove conjectures involving **properties of quadrilaterals**
- Learn the term **lemma**

You can prove many quadrilateral theorems by using triangle theorems. For example, you can prove some parallelogram properties by using the fact that a diagonal divides a parallelogram into two congruent triangles. This fact is an example of a **lemma**. A lemma is an auxiliary theorem used specifically to prove other theorems. The proof of the lemma is given as an example in your book. Write your own proof and then compare it to the one in the book. Call the lemma the Parallelogram Diagonal Lemma and add it to your list of theorems.

## Developing Proof: Proving Parallelogram Conjectures

In this activity you will prove three of your previous conjectures about parallelograms. Remember to draw a diagram, restate what is given and what you must show in terms of your diagram, and then make a plan before you write your proof.

Complete Step 1 in your book. (*Hint:* The proof will be a snap if you use the Parallelogram Diagonal Lemma.)

Now complete Step 2. (Don't forget the lemma!)

Step 3 asks you to state and prove the converse of the Opposite Sides Conjecture. The five-task proof process is started below.

Task 1: Identify what is given and what you must show.

**Given:**     A quadrilateral with opposite sides that are congruent

**Show:**     The quadrilateral is a parallelogram

Task 2: Draw and label a diagram to illustrate the given information.

Task 3: Restate the given and show information in terms of the diagram.

**Given:**     Quadrilateral $ABCD$ with $\overline{AD} \cong \overline{BC}$ and $\overline{AB} \cong \overline{DC}$

**Show:**     $ABCD$ is a parallelogram

Task 4: Make a plan.

Try to make a plan yourself. Here are some hints to get you started:

- So far all the quadrilateral proofs have involved drawing a diagonal to form triangles. Consider using that approach here.
- You need to show that the opposite sides of $ABCD$ are parallel. Look back and find theorems and postulates that can be used to prove that two lines are parallel. Which one do you think would be most useful in this situation?
- How can the triangle congruence postulates help you in your proof?

(continued)

Task 5: Write a proof.

You're on your own for this one!

Step 4 asks you to create a family tree for the theorems you proved in this investigation. See if you can fill in the blanks in the partially finished tree below.

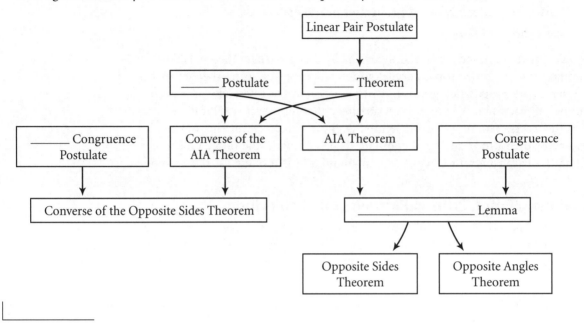

The following example is Exercise 2 in your book.

**EXAMPLE** | Prove the Opposite Sides Parallel and Congruent Conjecture: If one pair of opposite sides of a quadrilateral are parallel and congruent, then the quadrilateral is a parallelogram.

▶ **Solution** | **Given:** $\overline{WZ} \parallel \overline{XY}$; $\overline{WZ} \cong \overline{XY}$

**Show:** $WXYZ$ is a parallelogram

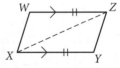

| Statement | Reason |
|---|---|
| **1.** Construct $\overline{XZ}$ | **1.** Line Postulate |
| **2.** $\overline{WZ} \parallel \overline{XY}$ | **2.** Given |
| **3.** $\angle WZX \cong \angle YXZ$ | **3.** AIA Theorem |
| **4.** $\overline{WZ} \cong \overline{XY}$ | **4.** Given |
| **5.** $\overline{XZ} \cong \overline{XZ}$ | **5.** Reflexive property of congruence |
| **6.** $\triangle WXZ \cong \triangle YZX$ | **6.** SAS Congruence Postulate |
| **7.** $\angle WXZ \cong \angle YZX$ | **7.** CPCTC |
| **8.** $\overline{WX} \parallel \overline{ZY}$ | **8.** Converse of the AIA Theorem |
| **9.** $WXYZ$ is a parallelogram | **9.** Definition of parallelogram |

# 13.5 Indirect Proof

In this lesson you will

- Learn to how to prove mathematical statements **indirectly**

Consider this multiple-choice question:

Which person twice won a Nobel prize?

   **A.** Sherlock Holmes

   **B.** Leonardo da Vinci

   **C.** Marie Curie

   **D.** Tiger Woods

You may not know the answer off the top of your head, but you can try to eliminate choices until only one possibility remains. Sherlock Holmes cannot be the correct answer because he is a fictional character. Leonardo da Vinci died long before Nobel prizes were awarded. Because there is no Nobel prize for golf, you can also eliminate Tiger Woods. That leaves one possibility, Marie Curie. Choice C must be the answer.

The type of thinking you used to answer the multiple-choice question is known as *indirect reasoning*. You can use this same type of reasoning to write an **indirect proof** of a mathematical statement.

For a given mathematical statement, there are two possibilities: Either the statement is true or it is not true. To prove indirectly that a statement is true, you start by assuming it is not true. You then use logical reasoning to show that this assumption leads to a contradiction. If an assumption leads to a contradiction, it must be false. Therefore, you can eliminate the possibility that the statement is not true. This leaves only one possibility—namely, that the statement is true!

Examples A and B in your book illustrate how an indirect proof works. Read these examples carefully. The example below is Exercise 7 in your book.

**EXAMPLE** | Prove that in a scalene triangle, the median cannot be the altitude.

▶ **Solution** | **Given:**      Scalene triangle *ABC* with median $\overline{CD}$

        **Show:**      $\overline{CD}$ is not the altitude to $\overline{AB}$

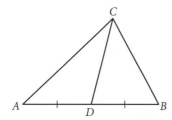

(continued)

| Statement | Reason |
|---|---|
| **1.** Assume $\overline{CD}$ *is* the altitude to $\overline{AB}$ | **1.** Assume the statement is *not* true |
| **2.** $\angle CDA$ and $\angle CDB$ are right angles | **2.** Definition of altitude |
| **3.** $\angle CDA \cong \angle CDB$ | **3.** Right Angles Congruent Theorem |
| **4.** $\overline{CD}$ is a median | **4.** Given |
| **5.** $\overline{AD} \cong \overline{BD}$ | **5.** Definition of median |
| **6.** $\overline{CD} \cong \overline{CD}$ | **6.** Reflexive property of congruence |
| **7.** $\triangle CDA \cong \triangle CDB$ | **7.** SAS Congruence Postulate |
| **8.** $\overline{CA} \cong \overline{CB}$ | **8.** CPCTC |

But the statement $\overline{CA} \cong \overline{CB}$ contradicts the fact that $\triangle ABC$ is scalene. Thus, the assumption that $\overline{CD}$ is the altitude to $\overline{AB}$ is false. Therefore, $\overline{CD}$ is *not* the altitude to $\overline{AB}$.

In Chapter 6, you discovered the Tangent Conjecture, which states that a tangent of a circle is perpendicular to the radius drawn to the point of tangency. In the developing proof activity you will prove this conjecture and its converse indirectly.

## Developing Proof: Proving the Tangent Conjecture

The activity in your book leads you through the steps of an indirect proof of the Tangent Conjecture. Complete the investigation on your own and then compare your answers to those below. Steps 9 and 10 are left for you to complete on your own.

**Step 1**  Perpendicular Postulate

**Step 2**  Segment Duplication Postulate

**Step 3**  Line Postulate

**Step 4**  Two reasons: $\angle ABO$ and $\angle CBO$ are right angles because of the definition of perpendicular. $\angle ABO \cong \angle CBO$ because of the Right Angles Congruent Theorem.

**Step 5**  Reflexive property of congruence

**Step 6**  SAS Congruence Postulate

**Step 7**  CPCTC

**Step 8**  It is given that $\overleftrightarrow{AT}$ *is* a tangent.

After you have completed the investigation, add the Tangent Theorem and its converse to your list of theorems.

# 13.6  Circle Proofs

In this lesson you will

- Learn the **Arc Addition Postulate**
- Prove conjectures involving properties of circles

Read Lesson 13.6 in your book. It introduces the Arc Addition Postulate and verifies that the Inscribed Angle Conjecture can now be called a theorem. The examples below are Exercises 1 and 2 in your book. For each example, write the proofs yourself before reading the solutions.

**EXAMPLE A**  Prove the Inscribed Angles Intercepting Arcs Conjecture: Inscribed angles that intercept the same or congruent arcs are congruent.

▸ **Solution**  Break the statement into two cases.

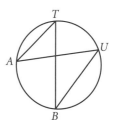

**Case 1:** The angles intercept the same arc.

**Given:**  $\angle A$ and $\angle B$ intercept $\overset{\frown}{TU}$

**Show:**  $\angle A \cong \angle B$

**Paragraph Proof**

By the Inscribed Angle Theorem, $m\angle A = \frac{1}{2}m\overset{\frown}{TU}$ and $m\angle B = \frac{1}{2}m\overset{\frown}{TU}$. By the transitive property of equality, $m\angle A = m\angle B$. By the definition of congruent angles, $\angle A \cong \angle B$.

**Case 2:** The angles intercept congruent arcs.

**Given:**  $\angle A$ intercepts $\overset{\frown}{MN}$; $\angle B$ intercepts $\overset{\frown}{PQ}$; $\overset{\frown}{MN} \cong \overset{\frown}{PQ}$

**Show:**  $\angle A \cong \angle B$

**Paragraph Proof**

Because $\overset{\frown}{MN} \cong \overset{\frown}{PQ}$, $m\overset{\frown}{MN} = m\overset{\frown}{PQ}$ by the definition of congruent arcs. By the multiplication property, $\frac{1}{2}m\overset{\frown}{MN} = \frac{1}{2}m\overset{\frown}{PQ}$. By the Inscribed Angle Theorem, $m\angle A = \frac{1}{2}m\overset{\frown}{MN}$ and $m\angle B = \frac{1}{2}m\overset{\frown}{PQ}$. Therefore, by the transitive property, $m\angle A = m\angle B$. By the definition of congruent angles, $\angle A \cong \angle B$.

(continued)

**EXAMPLE B** | Prove the Cyclic Quadrilateral Conjecture: The opposite angles of an inscribed quadrilateral are supplementary.

▸ **Solution** | **Given:** $\quad\quad\quad$ *ABCD* is inscribed in circle *O*

**Show:** $\quad\quad\quad$ $\angle A$ and $\angle C$ are supplementary;
$\quad\quad\quad\quad\quad$ $\angle B$ and $\angle D$ are supplementary

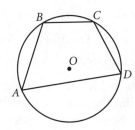

| **Statement** | **Reason** |
|---|---|
| **1.** $m\angle A = \frac{1}{2}m\widehat{BD}$; $\quad\quad m\angle C = \frac{1}{2}m\widehat{BAD}$ | **1.** Inscribed Angle Theorem |
| **2.** $m\angle A + m\angle C = \frac{1}{2}m\widehat{BD} + \frac{1}{2}m\widehat{BAD}$ | **2.** Addition property |
| **3.** $m\angle A + m\angle C = \frac{1}{2}(m\widehat{BD} + m\widehat{BAD})$ | **3.** Distributive property |
| **4.** $m\angle A + m\angle C = \frac{1}{2}($arc measure of circle $O)$ | **4.** Arc Addition Postulate |
| **5.** $m\angle A + m\angle C = \frac{1}{2}(360°) = 180°$ | **5.** Definition of arc measure of circle |
| **6.** $m\angle A$ and $m\angle C$ are supplementary | **6.** Definition of supplementary |

The steps above can be repeated for $\angle B$ and $\angle D$. Therefore, the opposite angles of *ABCD* are supplementary.

# 13.7 Similarity Proofs

**CONDENSED LESSON**

In this lesson you will

- Learn **properties of similarity**
- Prove conjectures involving similarity

The properties of equality and congruence can be extended to similarity. Read the properties of similarity on page 730 of your book. To prove similarity conjectures, you need to add the AA Similarity Postulate (formerly, the AA Similarity Conjecture) to the list of postulates. This postulate is stated in your book.

The example in your book shows how to use the AA Similarity Postulate to prove the SAS Similarity Conjecture. The proof is rather tricky, so read it carefully, following along with pencil and paper. Note that to get from Step 6 to Step 7, *DE* is substituted for *PB* in the denominator of the left ratio. This can be done because *P* was located so that $PB = DE$.

Below are the algebraic operations needed to get from Step 9 to Step 10.

$$\frac{BC}{BQ} = \frac{BC}{EF} \qquad \text{Step 9.}$$

$$EF \cdot BC = BQ \cdot BC \qquad \text{Multiply both sides by } BQ \cdot EF.$$

$$EF = BQ \qquad \text{Divide both sides by } BC.$$

Once you have worked through the example and understand it, add the SAS Similarity Theorem to your theorem list.

## Developing Proof: Proving the SSS Similarity Conjecture

In this activity you will prove the SSS Similarity Conjecture: If the three sides of one triangle are proportional to the three sides of another triangle, then the two triangles are similar.

**Given:** Two triangles with corresponding sides proportional

**Show:** The two triangles are similar

What you are given and what you must show are stated in terms of the diagram shown at right.

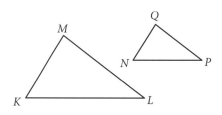

**Given:** $\triangle KLM$ and $\triangle NPQ$ with $\frac{KL}{NP} = \frac{LM}{PQ} = \frac{MK}{QN}$

**Show:** $\triangle KLM \sim \triangle NPQ$

Write a plan for the proof. (*Hint:* Use an auxiliary line like the one in the example in your book.) After you have written your plan, compare it to the one below.

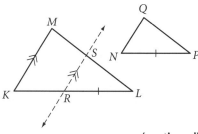

**Plan:** To show that $\triangle KLM \sim \triangle NPQ$, you need to show that one pair of corresponding angles is congruent. (We will show that $\angle L \cong \angle P$.) Then you can use the SAS Similarity Theorem to prove the triangles are similar. Use the same approach used in the example. Locate a point *R* on *KL* such that $RL = NP$. Then, through *R*, construct a line $\overleftrightarrow{RS}$ parallel to $\overline{KM}$.

(continued)

From the CA Postulate, $\angle SRL \cong \angle K$ and $\angle RSL \cong \angle M$. This means that $\triangle KLM \sim \triangle RLS$ by the AA Similarity Postulate. Now, if you can show that $\triangle RLS \cong \triangle NPQ$, then $\angle L \cong \angle P$ by CPCTC. Because $\triangle KLM \sim \triangle RLS$, then $\frac{KL}{RL} = \frac{LM}{LS} = \frac{MK}{SR}$ by the definition of similar triangles (CSSTP). Substituting $NP$ for $RL$ gives $\frac{KL}{NP} = \frac{LM}{LS} = \frac{MK}{SR}$.

Combining this with the given fact that $\frac{KL}{NP} = \frac{LM}{PQ} = \frac{MK}{QN}$, you can get the proportions $\frac{LM}{PQ} = \frac{LM}{LS}$ and $\frac{MK}{QN} = \frac{MK}{SR}$. Using some algebra gives $LS = PQ$ and $SR = QN$. So, $\triangle RLS \cong \triangle NPQ$ by the SSS Congruence Postulate. Thus, $\angle L \cong \angle P$ by CPCTC, so $\triangle KLM \sim \triangle NPQ$ by the SAS Similarity Theorem.

Step 4 gives part of a two-column proof. Fill in the missing reasons, and then write the steps and reasons needed to complete the proof. Compare your completed proof to the one below.

| Statement | Reason |
|---|---|
| **1.** Locate $R$ such that $RL = NP$ | **1.** Segment Duplication Postulate |
| **2.** Construct $\overleftrightarrow{RS} \parallel \overline{KM}$ | **2.** Parallel Postulate |
| **3.** $\angle SRL \cong \angle K$ | **3.** CA Postulate |
| **4.** $\angle RSL \cong \angle M$ | **4.** CA Postulate |
| **5.** $\triangle KLM \sim \triangle RLS$ | **5.** AA Similarity Postulate |
| **6.** $\frac{KL}{RL} = \frac{LM}{LS} = \frac{MK}{SR}$ | **6.** CSSTP (Definition of similar triangles) |
| **7.** $\frac{KL}{NP} = \frac{LM}{LS}$ | **7.** Substitution property of equality |
| **8.** $\frac{KL}{NP} = \frac{LM}{PQ}$ | **8.** Given |
| **9.** $\frac{KL}{NP} = \frac{MK}{SR}$ | **9.** Substitution property of equality |
| **10.** $\frac{KL}{NP} = \frac{MK}{QN}$ | **10.** Given |
| **11.** $\frac{LM}{LS} = \frac{LM}{PQ}$ | **11.** Transitive property of equality |
| **12.** $LS = PQ$ | **12.** Multiplication and division properties of equality |
| **13.** $\frac{MK}{SR} = \frac{MK}{QN}$ | **13.** Transitive property of equality |
| **14.** $SR = QN$ | **14.** Multiplication and division properties of equality |
| **15.** $\overline{LS} \cong \overline{PQ}$, $\overline{SR} \cong \overline{QN}$, $\overline{RL} \cong \overline{NP}$ | **15.** Definition of congruence |
| **16.** $\triangle RLS \cong \triangle NPQ$ | **16.** SSS Congruence Postulate |
| **17.** $\angle L \cong \angle P$ | **17.** CPCTC |
| **18.** $\triangle KLM \sim \triangle NPQ$ | **18.** SAS Similarity Theorem |

**Key Curriculum Press**
Innovators in Mathematics Education

# Comment Form

Please take a moment to provide us with feedback about this book. We are eager to read any comments or suggestions you may have. Once you've filled out this form, simply fold it along the dotted lines and drop it in the mail. We'll pay the postage. Thank you!

Your Name _____

School _____

School Address _____

City/State/Zip _____

Phone _____ Email _____

Book Title _____

Please list any comments you have about this book.

_____
_____
_____
_____
_____
_____
_____
_____
_____
_____
_____

Do you have any suggestions for improving the student or teacher material?

_____
_____
_____
_____
_____
_____
_____
_____

To request a catalog or place an order, call us toll free at 800-995-MATH or send a fax to 800-541-2242. For more information, visit Key's website at www.keypress.com.

Fold carefully along this line.

NO POSTAGE
NECESSARY
IF MAILED
IN THE
UNITED STATES

**Key Curriculum Press**
Innovators in Mathematics Education

Attn: Editorial Department
1150 65th Street
Emeryville, CA 94608-9740

Fold carefully along this line.

**Key Curriculum Press**

Innovators in Mathematics Education

# Comment Form

Please take a moment to provide us with feedback about this book. We are eager to read any comments or suggestions you may have. Once you've filled out this form, simply fold it along the dotted lines and drop it in the mail. We'll pay the postage. Thank you!

Your Name _____

School _____

School Address _____

City/State/Zip _____

Phone _____ Email _____

Book Title _____

Please list any comments you have about this book.

_____
_____
_____
_____
_____
_____
_____
_____
_____
_____
_____

Do you have any suggestions for improving the student or teacher material?

_____
_____
_____
_____
_____
_____
_____
_____

To request a catalog or place an order, call us toll free at 800-995-MATH or send a fax to 800-541-2242. For more information, visit Key's website at www.keypress.com.

Fold carefully along this line.

Fold carefully along this line.